ADVANCE PRAISE FOR *THE LAZY GOURMET*

"Whether you're a nervous newbie or a skilled cook with utmost confidence, you're sure to appreciate this smart recipe collection that allows you to put an impressive spread on the table even when you're pressed—which for most of us, is 24-7. With *The Lazy Gourmet*, co Imagine that."

— Carolyn Jung, James Beard Award-winning food

"I have always considered myself a lazy chef. For me, that means choosing seasonal, local ingredients, and relying on simple preparations to allow those ingredients to shine. In *The Lazy Gourmet*, Robin and Juliana have taken this approach to a whole new level, transforming 'lazy' into 'quintessentially elegant.'"

— John Scharffenberger, founder of Scharffen Berger Chocolate Maker

"Whether you're new to the kitchen or an experienced home chef, you'll love *The Lazy Gourmet*. With its good-humored approach, engaging style, useful culinary information, and delightfully easy and delicious recipes, it takes the stress out of cooking. If you want to prepare sophisticated, exceptional meals for your friends and family but are busy, kitchen-phobic, or just plain lazy, this is the cookbook for you."

— Sally Bernstein, editor-in-chief of Sally's Place, www.sallybernstein.com

"That cooking is fun is one of the best-kept secrets in some circles, but not here. With infectious enthusiasm, *The Lazy Gourmet* will inspire both the neophyte and the well-seasoned home cook toward making meals that show how easy it is to love cooking from scratch."

— Cheryl Koehler, editor and publisher of *Edible East Bay*

"Each member of my family is very social; we have people dropping by frequently. I often need to pull together a quick meal to share with our dear friends, so *The Lazy Gourmet* is now my go-to resource for marvelous recipes that 'impress for less.'"

— Billee Sharp, author of *Fix It, Make It, Grow It, Bake It*

"I LOVE to entertain and I am always searching for great recipes. Juliana Gallin and Robin Donovan have created delicious recipes and easy ideas for parties I will be using for many years. *The Lazy Gourmet* brings the fun back into the kitchen and puts it right on the table."

– Nina Lesowitz, coauthor of *The Party Girl Cookbook* and *Living Life as a Thank You*

THE lazy GOURMET

Magnificent Meals Made Easy

THE lazy GOURMET

Magnificent Meals Made Easy

by Robin Donovan and Juliana Gallin

Foreword by Joanne Weir

ViVa
EDITIONS

Published in the United States by Viva Editions, an imprint of
Cleis Press Inc., 2246 Sixth Street, Berkeley CA 94710.

Printed in the United States.
Cover design: Scott Idleman/Blink
Cover photograph: Getty Images: Fuse, Rachel Weill, Eriko Koga, Inti St. Clair, and Maren Caruso
Text design: Frank Wiedemann
First Edition.
10 9 8 7 6 5 4 3 2 1

Trade paper ISBN: 978-1-57344-653-2
E-book ISBN: 978-1-57344-674-7

Library of Congress Cataloging-in-Publication Data

Donovan, Robin.
  The lazy gourmet : magnificent meals made easy / by Robin Donovan and Juliana Gallin ; foreword, by Joanne Weir.
      p. cm.
  ISBN 978-1-57344-653-2 (pbk. : alk. paper)
  1. Quick and easy cooking. 2. Cookbooks. I. Gallin, Juliana. II. Title.
  TX833.5.D66 2011
  641.5'55--dc22
                              2010053399

Table of Contents

FOREWORD

Everyone has a talent. Some people are excellent doctors, some people love to design clothing. There are folks who make good architects and those who find pleasure and excel as scientists. Me? There's no question, I love to cook! And I love to teach people how to cook. I know it's not rocket science, but it takes patience, hard work, logic, common sense, and a few good cooking skills.

Cooking comes easily to me. I'm a fourth-generation chef. My mother was a professional cook, working at a private school planning menus and testing recipes. My grandfather cooked for summer boarders from New York City who came to experience life on a big dairy farm in the Berkshire Hills of Massachusetts. And then there was my great-grandmother.... Grandma Coulson was a wonderful all-American cook in a Boston restaurant called Pilgrim's Pantry at the turn of the 20th century. For me, there is no doubt, the art of cooking and love of food are deeply ingrained in my soul.

I always say there are two kinds of cooks in the world: those who love to cook because their mother or someone in their family instilled the love of food and cooking in them—that's me!—and those whose mother just didn't have the knack and furthermore had absolutely zero interest in the kitchen. Out of necessity and interest, the latter kind learns to cook for salvation and hopefully learns to love it.

That's my objective on my cooking show, *Joanne Weir's Cooking Class*. I take regular people who love food but are afraid to cook, don't know how to cook, or lack confidence in the kitchen. I teach these students how to make simple dishes that seem complicated. I love this process of standing side by side with students and seeing them go from saying they "can't cook" to being amazed and proud of their results. There's that wonderful "aha" moment when a student says, "I made this—and it's delicious! I can do it."

But no matter where your expertise and interest in cooking lies, there's a reason why you picked up this book. Obviously you love food, or at least you have an interest in the subject. Either you want to find out what cooking is all about or you want to pick up a few new great recipes to try out on your friends and family. Maybe you want to spend a little more time in the kitchen and hone your culinary skills.

Congratulations! You've come to the right place. This book is filled with food that's simple, seasonal, fresh, and doable. Here you'll find recipes that are perfect for family dinner on Tuesday night but fun, hip, and cool enough to serve your friends when you're entertaining on Saturday evening. And it's easy enough for even the novice to do.

All you'll need is a good set of knives, a cutting board, a few bowls, a stove, and some good fresh ingredients. The rest is all about patience—and following the recipes and pointers that lie between the covers of this book. You can do it! Remember, it's not rocket science. You can have a really fun time in the process.

Joanne Weir

INTRODUCTION

From the day the two of us met—as college students moving into a big drafty Victorian in Santa Cruz, California—we bonded over food. There were seven women living in the house, including science majors, banjo players, artists, and athletes. We were all very different, but the one thing we agreed on was food. We each contributed a set amount of cash to the food fund each week, and we took turns shopping and cooking dinner. Of course, we were barely out of our teens, and on student budgets, so the food was anything but fancy, but it was good enough to bring the seven of us—and a nightly assortment of friends, boyfriends, classmates, and random hangers-on—together around the dining room table most nights. There were, of course, plenty of frozen gnocchi and burritos, but there was also "homemade" calzone using store-bought pizza dough; a legendary rich, cream-based corn and tomato soup adapted from a recipe in *The Moosewood Cookbook*; and one July evening, when turkeys were inexplicably on sale for an irresistible price, an entire Thanksgiving feast, complete with bread stuffing, green bean casserole, and pumpkin pie. At best, there were homemade pierogies from someone's grandmother's recipe. At worst there was a terribly misguided sauté of nopales (Mexican cactus) that, to our dismay, even half a bottle of soy sauce couldn't save.

While we shared food costs and cooking duties—and a love of eating—our culinary knowledge was anything but equal, with the two of us at opposite ends of the spectrum. Robin, on the one hand, grew up in a food-obsessed family where the primary topic of dinner table conversation was where and what the next meal would be. Having grown up watching (and helping) her mother, a professional restaurant critic and accomplished cook, prepare dinner each night, cooking came naturally to her; she was simply comfortable in the kitchen, not intimidated by complicated recipes or exotic ingredients.

While Robin inherited her mother's kitchen prowess, Juliana, in contrast, cruised through childhood blissfully delighted when meals magically appeared in front of her. While she did master the Toll House cookie at a tender young age, she was generally more interested in eating than cooking. Pringles, candy bars, and four-star meals were all welcomed with equal enthusiasm. Frankly, she never gave cooking much thought until early adulthood, when she was ready to start preparing meals for herself and others. She was beginning to develop an appreciation for good food, but chalked the gourmet cooking abilities of others up to innate magical powers that she simply wasn't lucky enough to possess. She watched with bemusement as friends like Robin took seemingly random piles of meat and produce, mysterious powders, and liquids and transformed them into feasts that caused awestruck guests to burst into spontaneous applause. She wanted to be able to impress friends with dinner party spreads they would still be talking about months later, but she was resigned to the belief that she wasn't cut out to be a cooking whiz.

After college, Robin worked at a series of day jobs in the book publishing industry, and devoted the majority of her spare time to indulging her foodie urges. She devoured food magazines and television cooking shows, took cooking classes, and mastered complicated techniques. Both zealous and disciplined, she became known for her willingness to spend an entire week before a dinner party infusing oils, brining meats, and scouring markets throughout the San Francisco Bay Area in search of just the right ingredients. Eventually, she justified this devotion (read: obsession) by becoming a professional food writer, finally getting paid to ferret out delightfully minute culinary details for magazine and newspaper articles and develop recipes for her own cookbooks.

Juliana became a graphic designer and continued to passively enjoy the stellar culinary offerings of the Bay Area. While part of her always coveted her friends' cooking know-how, she couldn't imagine putting in the time, energy, and training she thought would be required for her to learn to cook great food. Eventually, though, it began to dawn on her that some of the most elegant, beautiful, and memorable meals she encountered—those that made foodies swoon, squeal, and beg for recipes—were also some of simplest. A surprising combination of unlikely ingredients, the use of fresh herbs, or a dash of a special vinegar or infused oil was often the thing that elevated a meal from decent to stunning. After years of befuddlement and self-doubt, Juliana had finally discovered a startling concept that changed the way she approached the kitchen: cooking great food can be really easy.

Over the years, the two of us frequently crammed ourselves into one or the other of our tiny, ill-equipped San Francisco apartment kitchens to cook and eat. As our lives became increasingly complicated and busy, more and more we both found ourselves looking for kitchen shortcuts that wouldn't oblige us to skimp on flavor. We'd make excited phone calls or send urgent late-night emails to share new recipes for super-delicious dishes, recipes that were "so easy!" Some of those recipes became legendary for us, like the ridiculously simple balsamic syrup that could transform the most mundane ingredients into culinary nirvana on a plate, or the egg and asparagus sandwich that earned one of us such a reputation at her workplace that we now refer to it as "THE sandwich."

We wrote *The Lazy Gourmet* for anyone who dreams of dazzling guests with fabulous home-cooked fare but fears that such a feat would require Thomas Keller's talent, Martha Stewart's ingenuity, Gandhi's patience, and Charles Manson's free time. Our goal is to conquer the misguided belief that preparing an elegant meal requires spending hours—or days—in the kitchen. With the help of our volunteer testers—regular people with no culinary training—we've developed this collection of recipes that can be prepared using readily available ingredients and common kitchen appliances, and without any previous cooking experience or training. With our recipes, we're confident that anyone can prepare delicious and sophisticated yet surprisingly simple dishes that will impress fussy in-laws, placate implacable bosses, and seduce sexy strangers through the proven method of knocking their socks off at the dinner table.

As we like to say, "Cooking a great meal can be just as easy as cooking a crappy meal!" So relax! Stop fretting over elaborate recipes and cumbersome techniques and start cooking the Lazy Gourmet way.

Part 1:
The Basics

Chapter One

PARTY IN YOUR PANTRY

A well-stocked kitchen makes Lazy Gourmet cooking a breeze. By keeping a few key ingredients on hand, you'll be able to turn the mundane into the magical on a moment's notice. Tired of standard salads? Toss in some roasted nuts and dried berries. Bored of bland eggs? Scramble in some capers and feta cheese. Startled by surprise guests? Whip up some Olive and Sun-Dried Tomato Tapenade (page 46) made from ingredients you just happen to have lying around and they'll think you were expecting them all along. (Watch out—they may begin to make a habit of dropping by unannounced and hungry.)

This chapter reveals our favorite pantry-, fridge-, and freezer-stocking items. Everything listed here has a reasonably long shelf life (ranging from a week or so to nearly infinite), making your well-stocked gourmet kitchen practically effortless to maintain.

BALSAMIC VINEGAR

This rich, sweet-tart Italian vinegar was so cherished in the olden days that it was sometimes included in the dowries of noblewomen and bequeathed in wills. It was even used, once upon a time, as a disinfectant and pain remedy. We can't vouch for its ability to sanitize bathrooms or cure tennis elbow, but we *can* attest to its deliciousness.

This versatile culinary treasure is used in salad dressings, sauces, marinades—even desserts and beverages. Splash it into a dish of olive oil and you've got a tasty dipping sauce for crusty bread. Or boil it down to a syrupy reduction (page 147) and drizzle it over roasted vegetables, meat, cheese, fruit, or ice cream.

Authentic, high-quality balsamic vinegar is aged for years in a secret progression of wooden barrels, each type of wood lending a particular aroma to the finished product. While the best balsamic vinegars have been aged a hundred years or more, luxurious and somewhat more afford-able 12-year-old versions are readily available in specialty food shops and high-end supermarkets. For the budget conscious, there are plenty of less expensive though still delicious versions available. Some may be made from red wine vinegar, aged in stainless steel tanks, or colored with caramel, but they still make for a tasty, multipurpose kitchen staple.

BROTH OR STOCK

Wondering what to do with that lonely head of cauliflower? Those last few carrots? If you've got a couple of cans of broth on hand (as well as an onion and some basic spices) you can whip up beautiful gourmet soups without having to set foot outside the house—a perfect solution for the epicurean agoraphobe. We like to keep a variety of broths around, including vegetable, chicken, beef, and fish or shellfish. Leftover broth can be stored in the refrigerator, in a tightly sealed container, for up to a week.

CAPERS

These mysterious little green balls, ranging in size from pea to olive, are the unripened flower buds of *Capparis spinosa,* a prickly bush native to the Mediterranean. Preserved in wine vinegar or brine, they have a tart, tangy flavor, and add a surprising complexity to sauces, salads, fish, chicken dishes, and even sandwiches. Because capers are pickled, they'll last in the refrigerator, even after the jar has been opened, for months. For a sophisticated crunchy garnish, try deep-frying your capers.

CHEESE

In all its myriad glorious forms, cheese is without a doubt one of *the* most important staples of the lactose-tolerant Lazy Gourmet's kitchen. Here we list a few of our favorites to keep on hand.

Blue cheeses

Blue cheese is the general term for cow's milk, sheep's milk, or goat's milk cheeses that have had cultures added to cause the development of edible molds throughout the cheese. This delicacy was no doubt discovered by accident—a batch of cheese was left to age in a spooky French cave, grew moldy, and was eaten by some brave, hungry, unwitting culinary pioneer. These days, pungent, salty blue cheeses like Roquefort, Stilton, Maytag, Gorgonzola, and Blue Castello are created intentionally by adding mold spores to the cheese during production, and are prized by food connoisseurs around the world. Blue cheese is delicious in salads with fruit and nuts (see Pear, Escarole, and Blue Cheese Salad, page 57) or as an addition to savory baked goods (see Savory Blue Cheese Shortbread, page 38).

Chèvre

Chèvre (pronounced shev, at least by Americans) is the French word for "goat" and refers to the soft, fresh goat's milk cheese commonly found in supermarkets in the U.S. A label that reads "pur chèvre" guarantees a product made entirely from goat's milk; others may contain added cow's milk. While the texture and consistency of chèvres vary from producer to producer, chèvre found in the U.S. is most commonly comparable to a slightly dry cream cheese—with a richer, tangier flavor. Chèvre is delicious in salads and sandwiches (see Olive and Sun-Dried Tomato Tapenade Sandwich, page 87) or with chicken or pasta (see Pasta with Asparagus, Leeks, and Chèvre, page 102), or simply spread on a piece of hot French bread and topped with marinated sun-dried tomatoes. Wrapped tightly in plastic, chèvre will last in the refrigerator for a couple of weeks. Once past its prime, chèvre takes on a sour taste and should be tossed out.

Feta cheese

Just like Doric columns and democracy, feta cheese is a momentous Greek invention. Although it won't hold up your roof or give the common man a voice, it *will* make your salads delicious. Feta—Greek for "slice"—is traditionally made of sheep's or goat's milk, but today some commercial brands are made with cow's milk, creating a milder product. It ranges in texture from soft to semihard and crumbles easily. Cured and stored in salty brine, feta has a tart, tangy flavor that is irresistible in salads, on sautéed vegetables, or blended into a spread (see our Spicy Feta Spread, page 45). The brine also acts as a preservative, so feta doesn't spoil easily—precisely the point, as it was originally produced thousands of years before the era of refrigeration. A chunk of feta will keep in the refrigerator for a couple of weeks—even longer if you store it in its salty brine.

Hard cheeses

As they age, cheeses usually become firmer as well as more pungent, so hard cheeses are particularly flavorful. The common varieties Parmesan, Asiago, Pecorino, and Romano add a nearly compulsory savor and richness to pasta, risotto, soups, and salads—plus, they make a beautiful garnish when grated into a fine fluff or shaved into curls with a vegetable peeler. Italian Parmigiano-Reggiano, which is aged for a minimum of three years, is considered the best-quality Parmesan. Hard cheeses have long shelf lives—you can keep a block, tightly wrapped in plastic, in the refrigerator for months. If a spot of mold develops, just cut it away. To save time during dinner prep, you can grate or shave your cheese a couple of days in advance and store it in the refrigerator, in a tightly sealed container, until ready to use.

Mascarpone

This creamy, dense, high-fat cow's milk product is technically not a cheese, but is usually referred to as one, so we'll go ahead and brazenly include it here. Originating in Italy, mascarpone (pronounced mass-car-<u>poh</u>-nay) is often used in desserts like tiramisù, but can also be used to add richness and texture to savory dishes like our Spicy Crab Cakes (page 98) or Baked Polenta with Mascarpone and Corn (page 143). It has a soft, spreadable consistency comparable to cream cheese, which is a decent substitute—either on its own or combined in equal parts with sour cream—if you can't find mascarpone.

CHIPOTLE CHILES IN ADOBO SAUCE

Chipotle chiles are smoked jalapeños, usually sold canned in adobo sauce. They're fairly spicy with a distinctive smoky flavor that adds depth and richness to soups, stews, and sauces. We use them in a number of recipes, including Spicy Chicken Mole (page 120) and Roasted Potato Slices with Chipotle-Lime Sour Cream (page 50). You can find chipotle chiles in Latin American food stores or the Hispanic foods aisle of many supermarkets. Since you're probably not going to use an entire can, unless you're cooking mass quantities or are a masochist, store the remaining portion in an airtight container in the freezer and chip off frozen chile chunks as you need them—or better yet, put one chile with a healthy spoonful of the adobo sauce into each well of an ice cube tray and freeze overnight. Transfer the cubes to a ziplock plastic bag and pull out cubes as you need them.

CITRUS FRUITS

We're always sure to have a healthy reserve of citrus fruits—especially lemons, limes, and oranges—on hand for flavor emergencies. We use the juice to add sweetness or tang to salad dressings, marinades, sauces, dips, and spreads. The zest—the colored outer part of the peel—adds an extra boost of flavor when used with the juice, but it also provides intense citrus flavor when you don't want to add liquid (as in dry rubs, flavored salts, and some baked goods). When using zest, be sure to scrub the fruit well first, and then remove the zest with a Microplane grater (our preferred zesting tool), citrus zester, cheese grater, vegetable peeler, or sharp knife, being careful to avoid the bitter white pith beneath it. The flesh of citrus fruit makes a pretty addition to salads, desserts, and cheese plates.

Unrefrigerated, citrus fruits will last up to a couple of weeks. Stash them in your nice, cool crisper and their life span will increase dramatically. Warm or room temperature fruit yields more juice than refrigerated. A few seconds in the microwave can help you get the most out of fruit that has been refrigerated.

In our recipes we equate the juice of one lemon to about 3 tablespoons, the juice of one lime to about 1½ tablespoons, and the juice of one organge to about ¼ cup—but these numbers aren't set in stone. Adjust your quantities to the size and juiciness of your citrus fruits, as well as to your own taste.

Lemons

We use lemon juice and zest in everything from pasta sauces to cookies. We especially love Meyer lemons, which were brought from their native China to the U.S. in the early 20th century by plant explorer Frank Meyer. Believed to be a cross between regular lemons and Mandarin or sweet oranges, they are sweeter and juicier than the regular variety, and have a thin, edible skin. Thinly sliced, they make a gorgeous topping for pizza or savory tarts (see Meyer Lemon and Asparagus Tart, page 92).

Limes

Lime juice and zest are essential components of many South and Central American and Asian cuisines. Limes add a special tang to our Watermelon, Feta, and Mint Salad (page 65) and take center stage in our Wasabi-Lime Vinaigrette (page 151) and our Lime Dream Ice Cream (page 172).

Oranges

We like both the common navel orange and the uniquely flavored cara cara orange for adding bright sweetness to sauces, dressings, and desserts. Keep a couple on hand and you'll always be prepared to whip up our Orange Crème Fraîche Cake (page 184) on a moment's notice. Experiment with other varieties, like faintly raspberry-flavored blood oranges or sour Seville oranges.

CRÈME FRAÎCHE

Crème fraîche, which originated along the south coast of France, is now officially (according to us!) one of the modern world's most delicious dairy products. It's similar to sour cream, with a tart, creamy flavor, but is made with a lower amount of bacterial culture and has a thicker consistency. You'll find it used throughout this book in delectable recipes like Crème Fraîche and Buttermilk Ice Cream (page 174) and Orange Crème Fraîche Cake with Bittersweet Chocolate Drizzle (page 184), and as a suggested topping for various sweet and savory dishes. If you can't find crème fraîche, substitute sour cream.

DIJON MUSTARD

Excuse me, do you have any Grey Poupon? Well, you should. Dijon mustard is frequently used to add flavor to vinaigrettes, sauces, chicken, fish, cooked vegetables—and of course, hot dogs. Made from the seeds of a plant related to cabbages and radishes, mustard is one of the world's oldest flavorings, dating back at least 3,000 years. While the ancient Chinese, Greeks, Romans, and Egyptians all enjoyed the "condiment of kings" in one way or another, it was the city of Dijon, France, that rose to global mustard supremacy beginning in the 13th century. The strictly controlled Dijon recipe always uses brown or black seeds ground and mixed with wine or vinegar, which reacts with the seeds' oils to create that trademark sharp-tangy flavor. An exemplary fridge-stocking item, it'll last for ages, even after the jar is opened.

DRIED FRUIT

Our pantries are like miniature desiccated orchards, packed with all kinds of dehydrated fruits just waiting to be tossed into stews and baked into scones. Sweet dried fruits, like dates or apricots, are a perfect match for salty cheeses and dress up a cheese platter nicely. Tart dried cherries and blueberries add color and flair to a simple salad. Because of the high concentration of sugars and lack of water, dried fruits can last for ages without refrigeration—making them an ideal pantrystuffer. They're delicious as is, or they can be rehydrated in hot water to fill in for fresh fruit in recipes like our Fig and Onion Jam (page 158).

DRIED MUSHROOMS

Fresh wild mushrooms, while undeniably scrumptious, can really break the bank. Some wild mushrooms lose their appeal when dried (chanterelles, for instance, really don't hold up), but fortunately, many retain their delicious flavors—and some are even improved by the process. Dried porcinis, morels, and shiitakes can be found in most supermarkets. The price of the tiny packages may seem steep, but remember, the dehydration process concentrates the flavors, so a little goes a long way—a few ounces of dried mushrooms, once rehydrated, is usually enough to replace a pound of the fresh ones.

To rehydrate dried mushrooms, soak them in hot, but not boiling, water for 30 minutes. The soaking liquid will retain a good deal of rich mushroom flavor, so reserve it for use in sauces or risotto, or to use a soup stock.

FLAVORED OILS AND VINEGARS

These days oil and vinegar come infused with a dizzying array of flavors: Meyer lemon, raspberry, fig, red pepper, basil, roasted garlic, black truffle, and the list goes on. These bottled wonders are the ultimate secret weapon for Lazy Gourmets. Toss them with salad greens, marinate meat in them, or drizzle them over pasta. They offer intense, concentrated flavor right out of the bottle.

Drizzle Meyer lemon oil over seared scallops. Toss pasta with chunks of smoked chicken, crushed red pepper, and basil oil. Baste potatoes with roasted garlic oil, sprinkle with salt and pepper, and roast until crispy. With almost no added effort, mundane dishes are completely transformed.

To really fancify a dish, drizzle a bit of black or white truffle oil over it—just make sure to purchase a bottle with an ingredient list that actually includes truffles. The tiny bottles are expensive, but a little goes a long way and few things thrill foodies more than the word "truffled" preceding a dish.

Flavored vinegars offer countless variations on the green salad. For an elegant take on an old standby, dress mixed greens with a mixture of sherry or black fig vinegar, chopped shallots, olive oil, and salt and pepper, and sprinkle with crumbled blue cheese and toasted walnuts. Champagne vinegar, olive oil, and salt are all that's needed to dress a salad of mixed greens, avocado, and pink grapefruit sections.

The combinations are endless. Stock your cabinets with a wide variety of flavored oils and vinegars and you'll never run short of menu ideas.

GARLIC

In ancient Greece and Rome, garlic was used for medicinal purposes, believed to cure such diverse ailments as leprosy, asthma, and dog bites. Ancient Egyptians fed garlic to their slaves to increase their pyramid-building stamina. And in the Middle Ages the omnipotent little bulb was thought to prevent the Black Death. While modern science is revisiting the idea of garlic's curative properties—the possibility that it might be able to lower blood pressure and cholesterol, prevent cancer, and treat certain infections—we use it mostly to flavor our food and ward off vampires. It's even delicious all by itself, roasted until soft and spread on a good crusty bread (see Roasted Garlic, page 162). Garlic should be stored in a cool, dark, dry place—don't put it in the refrigerator or it will get soft and moldy. Unbroken bulbs will last for a couple of months; individual cloves, separated from the bulb, will last about a week.

HERBS, FRESH

While fresh herbs can't compete with pasta or vinegar for the Pantry Longevity Awards, they make up for it with their invaluable contributions in the categories of incomparable flavor, visual aesthetics, and all-around gourmet cachet. Meat, poultry, fish, soups, pasta, salads, breads, and even desserts can be enhanced by one fresh herb or another. Add dill or chives to salads; bake chicken with rosemary or sage; sauté mushrooms with thyme or tarragon; sprinkle cilantro leaves on a bowl of soup; garnish a dish of chocolate ice cream with a sprig of mint. You get the idea. Fresh herbs rock. Don't get us wrong—dried herbs are indispensable to the gourmet pantry, but they don't look as beautiful, and they simply taste different from their freshly picked former selves. While the drying process concentrates flavors and makes dried herbs taste stronger in some ways, it also causes some of the herbs' subtle flavors to be lost altogether. Because of this concentration, if you need to use a dried herb in place of fresh, use one-third the amount the recipe calls for. (So, for instance, one tablespoon of chopped fresh basil is equivalent to one teaspoon of dried basil.) And keep in mind that *new* dried herbs taste much stronger and better than those that have been sitting in your cupboard since college. So if you're using an older jar, bump up the quantity a bit.

If you don't have your own herb garden, effective storage is a matter of some concern, especially since you're almost always obliged to buy more of a fresh herb than you really need for any one dish. One good storage method is to wrap the cut ends of the herbs in a moist paper towel and refrigerate them in a perforated or partially open plastic bag. Another is to put the herbs in a jar of water, like a bouquet of flowers, and cover their tops loosely with a plastic bag. Sometimes herbs will last a good long time with no special attention—just bagged and refrigerated.

Keep in mind that the finer you chop fresh herbs, the more you release their flavor. And prolonged cooking causes fresh herbs to lose their fragrance and their flavor, so if possible (if you're not rubbing a roast, for example) add them in near the end of the cooking time.

NUTS

We absolutely never tire of our nutty little friends. Keep a variety of shelled nuts on hand to toss into salads and stir-frys, or serve them with cheese and olives for a no-fuss appetizer platter. You'll find the recipes in this book sprinkled with delectable pistachios, almonds, walnuts, peanuts, and pecans—but one of our all-time favorite ingredients is pine nuts (which are technically not even nuts, but seeds). Try this simple experiment: whatever you're planning to cook, add the phrase "with toasted pine nuts" to the end of the name. Doesn't that sound great? (It doesn't *always* work, but we trust you to use your best judgment.) These tiny, flavor-packed morsels are actually the edible seeds of several different species of pine tree—they live inside the pinecone, which is heated to facilitate the release of its delectable progeny. Most nuts are high in fat, so unless you're planning to consume them within a couple of months, store them in the fridge or freezer to keep them from becoming rancid.

Many recipes call for toasted nuts because heating brings out their flavor. You can either buy them pretoasted or toast them yourself using one of two easy methods: spread them in a single layer on a baking sheet and bake at 375°F until they're lightly browned (7 to 10 minutes), or stir them in a hot, dry skillet over medium heat until they're lightly browned (5 to 7 minutes). Pine nuts can burn quickly, so dial down the heat a bit for these sensitive little guys.

P.S. In the interest of full disclosure we must tell you that peanuts are actually not nuts but legumes, like peas and beans. Sorry if that freaks you out.

OLIVE OIL

Although there are many oils acceptable for cooking, olive oil is a time-tested classic prized around the world for its versatility, health benefits, and delicious flavor. Called "liquid gold" by Homer, the oil of pressed olives was used in antiquity to anoint the heads of nobles, coat athletes' bodies, and even honor the bones of dead saints. According to modern-day nutritionists, olive oil contains healthy monounsaturated fats, antioxidants, and even an anti-inflammatory agent—all of which may reduce the risk of a host of ills, from stroke to cancer to heart disease. As with wines, olive oils vary dramatically with the soil and climate of their growing regions as well as the variety of tree and time of harvest. Products can range from a light champagne color to bright green. In general, the deeper the color, the stronger the flavor.

All olive oils are graded in accordance with their degree of acidity. At the top of the line, with an acidity of only 1 percent, are those that are both *extra virgin* (traditionally the result of the first pressing of the olives) and *cold pressed* (a chemical-free pressing process). *Virgin* olive oil has an acidity level of about 2 percent. Today, the terms "first pressing" and "second pressing" are mostly anachronistic, as the vast majority of oil is made in continuous centrifugal presses—but the terms endure as an indication of acidity and quality. *Fino* is a blend of virgin and extra virgin. *Refined* oil has been treated to neutralize unpleasant tastes and acid content. *Pure* olive oil—or simply "olive oil"—is refined oil combined with virgin or extra virgin. *Light* olive oil contains the same amount of fat as traditional, but an extremely fine filtration process gives it a lighter flavor and color, making it mild enough for baking. It also has a higher smoke point, making it better for frying and other high-heat cooking, whereas regular olive oil is best for low- and medium-heat cooking. Flavorful extra virgin is the best choice for uncooked foods like salad dressings.

Olive oil can be stored in a cool, dark place for months. To double its life span you can keep it in the refrigerator, where it will become thick, cloudy, and unsightly—but will return to its normal liquid state when brought back up to room temperature.

OLIVE OR VEGETABLE OIL SPRAY

This tidy, time-saving product lets you oil pans for sautéing, grease cookie sheets for baking, coat veggies for roasting, and oil crostini for broiling with a mere twitch of an index finger. This is not your mother's nonstick mystery spray. These days, spray oils contain the same high-quality product that comes bottled, but give you much more control over its application. If you prefer a pump to aerosol, purchase an oil mister at a kitchen supply store and fill it with your favorite oil.

OLIVES

A simple jar of olives can be a real lifesaver. Perhaps not literally, like antibiotics or the Heimlich maneuver, but if you're dying for some deliciousness, olives are the cure. The bottled variety, cured in brine or oil, will sit patiently in your pantry until you're ready for them. Many supermarkets now offer "olive bars" that allow you to choose as many or as few as you want of different varieties—Greek, French, Italian, garlic-stuffed, pimiento-stuffed, oil-cured, spicy, herbed, and even liquored-up. Pick and choose to make your own unique olive combo to add to an antipasto platter, toss into a salad, top a pizza, or pop into swanky martinis. A staple of Mediterranean cuisine, olives are also a great way to get your heart-healthy monounsaturated fats.

ONIONS

Not only can you sauté, caramelize, roast, braise, fry, grill, or pickle these pungent little bulbs— you can also bury them with the next Pharaoh you have occasion to entomb. Or try using them as a medicine to promote healthy digestion, vision, and heart function, as did the ancient Indians. Or consume several pounds of them before your next Olympic competition, like an ancient Greek athlete. But even if you don't choose to use onions for spiritual, medicinal, or athletic purposes, you should always keep a couple around the kitchen for cooking—they add flavor and dimension to everything they encounter. You can even feature them solo—just peel, rub with olive oil, roast in the oven until soft, and drizzle with Balsamic Syrup (page 147) for a rustic side dish. Raw onions are hearty—they should last for a few weeks in a cool, dry, well-ventilated spot, away from direct sunlight. Chopped onions will keep in the refrigerator, in a tightly sealed container, for a couple of days.

PASTA, DRIED

While fresh pasta is a delicacy that we wholeheartedly recommend you consume whenever you can, dried pasta has been a vital feature of the Italian diet for centuries. Old prints and drawings show workshops draped with miles of spaghetti drying in the hot Mediterranean sun. It's hearty and nutritious, and its exceptionally long shelf life makes it a model member of any modern pantry.

To crank your gourmet status up a level, try some of the lesser-known types in place of the typical penne, linguine, and spaghetti. Black pasta, flavored and colored with squid ink, is delicious (not to mention beautiful) with seafood dishes. Pastas colored with carrot, spinach, beet, tomato, or squash also add a considerable dazzle factor to ordinary pasta dishes. Fregola, from the island of Sardinia, consists of tiny chewy balls made from coarsely ground semolina. It's delicious with sauces or in soups. Orzo and risi are tiny, smooth-textured, rice-shaped pastas that are wonderful in soups or served as a substitute for rice. Star-shaped stelle and square-shaped chilopitta both provide a nice visual break from the usual tubes and strands. Couscous is a delightful North African micropasta that resembles very large grains of sand.

Store your favorites pastas in an airtight container in a cool, dry place and they'll last a good long time.

PEPPERS, ROASTED AND JARRED

Roasted, jarred peppers (usually red) are a pantry must. An unopened jar of roasted peppers has a very long shelf life, waiting patiently in your cupboard until you're ready to enhance sandwiches, stews, sauces, and cheese platters with its delicious contents. And even once you've opened the jar, the peppers will stay fresh and usable in the fridge for another week or so. Roasting your own peppers isn't the world's most difficult task, but popping open a little glass jar is far easier.

PUFF PASTRY, FROZEN

The process of making puff pastry from scratch is complex and time-consuming, to say the least, and should not be attempted by a Lazy Gourmet for any reason. So how are you going to dazzle your friends by making extraordinary Apple, Blue Cheese, and Walnut Tarts (page 94)? Luckily, you can buy premade, frozen puff pastry sheets that are easy to use and result in a perfectly delightful finished product. If you can find it, shell out a few extra bucks for a top-quality brand that uses real butter; otherwise the standard supermarket brands will do just fine.

Here are a few tips for working with frozen puff pastry. To thaw, let the box sit at room temperature for 45 minutes. You can also thaw it in the fridge overnight and then let it sit out at room temperature for 10 minutes before using. When it is thawed and ready to use, gently unfold pastry sheet on a lightly floured surface. If there is any moisture on the dough from the thawing, blot it dry with a paper towel. If it tears or cracks along the fold lines, just pinch it together with your fingers and patch with a drop of water, if necessary. Prick the dough with a fork, at ½-inch intervals, before baking to prevent it from puffing up in the middle. But don't prick the areas that you *do* want to puff up, for example around the edge of a tart. And finally, if you want the exposed parts of the pastry to have a nice brown glaze, brush them with lightly beaten egg before baking.

RICE

We know what you're thinking: rice is rice, an utterly forgettable side dish, right? But did you know there are actually more than 40,000 different types of rice? If you haven't been down the rice aisle in your supermarket for a while, you may be surprised by the rainbow of grains you'll find there: green and black from China, red from France and the tiny Himalayan kingdom of Bhutan, black Italian, purple Thai, and countless other hues.

Indeed, the world of rice is as complex as that of fine wines, right down to the *terroir*—the unique combination of soil, climate, and altitude that gives each rice its own distinctive flavor and texture. Bhutanese red rice, for instance, is irrigated by mineral-heavy glacier water that gives it an earthy flavor. Another red rice, from France's marshy Camargue area, is mildly sweet. China's iron-rich "forbidden" black rice is nutty, smoky, and low in starch. Italian venere Piemontese combines the high starch content and large size of arborio (commonly used for risotto) with the ebony color and nuttiness of the Chinese black. Many of these rices are "heirloom" grains, meaning they're grown from seeds passed down for hundreds of years without being cross-bred or altered in any way. Keep a few of these exotic rices on hand and you'll be able to impress guests not only with their deliciousness, but also with tales of their ancient histories.

SALT

These days, you'll find a salt shaker on just about every table in America, and many other countries, too, but back in ancient times this mineral—a seasoning, a preservative, and a vital nutrient all at once—was a prized commodity, even used in some societies as currency. Today, copious amounts of salt are mined from large deposits left in long-dried lakes. Don't let salt's ubiquity fool you, though. Not all salt is created equal.

Kosher salt

Kosher salt isn't just for rabbis anymore—food connoisseurs swear by it. Because it's made without additives, it provides a clean, pure flavor chefs love. It's coarser than common table salt, so there's less of it in any given volume, giving the cook more control and making it harder to inadvertently oversalt food. Its coarseness also makes it very easy to pick up by the pinch. We specify kosher salt in most of our recipes. You'll find it in just about any supermarket, alongside the table salt.

When using kosher salt, remember that because of its large grains, it delivers less salt in any given volume than fine-grained table or sea salt. To complicate matters further, there are two common brands of kosher salt—Morton's and Diamond—and due to different manufacturing processes, wouldn't you know, they deliver surprisingly different amounts of salt by volume. Morton's is denser and more intensely salty than the lighter, flakier Diamond. We use Morton's kosher salt in our testing kitchens, so if you've got a different brand or type of salt in your kitchen, your dishes may end up underseasoned, but that's easily fixed by tasting and adjusting the seasoning as necessary—a whole lot easier than trying to take salt out of an overseasoned dish. As a general rule of thumb:

1 teaspoon table salt
= 1¼ teaspoons Morton's kosher salt
= 1¾ teaspoons Diamond kosher salt

Sea salt
Sea salt comes from evaporated seawater. These days, specialty shops sell sea salts from every corner of the world and each has its own distinct flavor and texture. If you're interested, try purchasing a few different sea salts and simply experiment with them.

Table (or iodized) salt
Table salt is fine-grained salt that has had sodium iodide (a crucial nutrient for preventing hypothyroidism) added to it. While true foodies spurn table salt as inferior to kosher or sea salts for most cooking, it is useful in baking, where its fine grain allows it to disperse more quickly and uniformly into other ingredients. We specify table salt in our baking recipes, but remember, when substituting table salt in recipes that call for kosher salt, be sure to reduce the amount. (See the formula above, under kosher salt.)

Whatever type of salt you choose, remember that this seasoning is one of the most important ingredients in just about any recipe. The truth is, salt doesn't just add saltiness. It tenderizes meat; draws moisture from vegetables, which aids in caramelization; and provides flavor balance, making sweet, sour, or bitter flavors more prominent. Salt is also still used as a preservative in many cuisines, in cured meats like bacon, pancetta, and prosciutto or in pickled vegetables.

SEAFOOD, FROZEN

Keep an emergency bag of shrimp, scallops, or mixed seafood in your freezer and you'll never find yourself wondering what to feed those last-minute dinner guests. You can thaw them out (the bags of seafood, not the guests) pretty quickly by placing the sealed bag in a bowl of cold water or emptying the seafood into a colander and running cold water over it until thawed completely. Broil prawns in a rich Romesco sauce (page 100) or bake chopped scallops with lemon juice, capers and herbs (page 96). Frozen fish can be used to whip up any one of our cooked fish recipes (not ceviche or other uncooked seafood dishes) on a moment's notice.

SUN-DRIED TOMATOES

Before the era of modern canning methods, Italians used to dry summer tomatoes on their tile roofs for use during the winter. Nowadays, sun-dried tomatoes are considered a delicacy any time of the year. While they won't win any beauty pageants, these wrinkly little devils deliver a powerful dose of concentrated flavor to pasta salads, sandwiches, and tomato-based sauces. Sun-dried tomatoes that have been rehydrated and marinated in olive oil are tender and more savory than the dry, packaged variety, but the jar must be refrigerated once it's opened. The dry-packed variety will sit patiently in your cupboard for months, allowing you to rehydrate just what you need when you need it. To do so, cover the dried tomatoes with boiling water and let soak until tender, about 10 to 15 minutes; or just cut them up and drop them right into soups and stews as they cook. Serve sun-dried tomatoes on homemade pizzas, as part of an antipasto platter, or as a topping for crispy goat cheese crostini.

WINE (FOR COOKING)

Always keep some inexpensive wine handy for cooking—but remember, you never want to cook with wine you wouldn't be happy to drink. Once you've opened the bottle, it's best to consume it as soon as possible. (We apologize in advance for any unnecessary drunkenness this advice may cause.) If you absolutely can't bear to drink it up by yourself and don't have a crew of surly sailors handy to help you out, cork it and store it in the refrigerator for up to two or three days. (We actually keep opened wine a whole lot longer, and off the record we're happy to advise you to do the same, but should the haute cuisine police get wind of such shenanigans we'll swear we never said any such thing.)

Sherry and port—which are fortified with brandy—are also clever tricks to keep up your culinary sleeve. Sherry adds a caramel-like sweetness and nutty flavor to sauces and soups and pairs especially well with cream and wild mushrooms. Always use sherry that is intended for drinking rather than products labeled "cooking sherry," which is really just cheap sherry with salt added. Port tends to be sweeter and fruitier than sherry and is ideal for making reduction sauces for duck, beef, or pork. We also like to soak berries in port and serve them over ice cream. Because of their high alcohol content, sherry and port can be kept for ages in sealed containers in a cool, dark place.

Chapter Two

TIPS FOR ROOKIE COOKS AND LAZY GOURMETS

What seems perfectly obvious to the experienced cook can scare a novice right out of the kitchen, so for those of you who are new to cooking, we've put together some tips, suggestions, and simple explanations that we hope will squelch your fears and make it the fun and satisfying adventure it is meant to be. We've also included our favorite Lazy Gourmet tips and shortcuts—tricks that will make cooking faster and easier. So whether you're a kitchen newbie or a lazy old pro, read this section to discover a tip or two that we hope will help you prepare easy, stress-free, delicious meals.

READ THE RECIPE
Before you begin cooking—even before you decide on something you think you'd like to make—read the whole recipe all the way through. Make sure you know up front if something needs to be made the day before and chilled overnight, or if it's best served straight out of the oven, or if it serves two people and you're expecting 10.

DON'T STRESS OVER QUANTITIES
"One teaspoon of ground cumin" is merely a suggestion. In fact, unless you're baking, when precise measurements truly do matter, most recipes are merely suggestions. Since this is a cookbook, as opposed to a conversation, we provide detailed instructions for making our dishes—but please take those instructions with a grain (or half a teaspoon) of salt. If you adore black pepper, or garlic, or beets, go ahead and use as much as you'd like, wantonly ignoring our recommendations. Just take care not to overdo it; taste as you go.

DON'T STRESS OVER INGREDIENTS

It may sound strange if you're used to following recipes word for word, but even ingredients are negotiable. If you're making a stuffed chicken breast recipe, then, yes, you do kind of need a chicken breast. But you don't need to follow any recipe (except when you're baking) precisely as written. If a recipe calls for three or four dried herbs and you've only got two of them, you don't need to run out to the market for those you don't have on hand. Just use what you have, increasing their quantities to make up for the missing flavors. You can even swap one dried herb for another—just sniff around your spice rack until your nose finds you a good substitute. Firm vegetables can often be used interchangeably—vegetables like broccoli, cauliflower, carrots, and potatoes. So can the more tender veggies—eggplant, peppers, mushrooms, asparagus. If a recipe calls for butternut squash, try swapping it with pumpkin, zucchini, or summer squash. Pretty much all salad greens are interchangeable, though the end result may have a slightly different look or flavor. A recipe that calls for a soft fruit like peaches will probably work just as well with another soft fruit, like apricots or pears. One nut or berry is as good as another. What we're trying to say is: Don't be afraid to experiment, whether inspired by creativity or by constraints!

FRESH VERSUS FROZEN

Whether we're talking about meat, fish, fruits, or vegetables, fresh is always preferable to frozen. Who wouldn't want to cook with ingredients purchased that morning at the farmer's market or picked straight from your bountiful garden? But we know that this scenario isn't always possible, so feel free to substitute frozen foods when necessary. In fact, the FDA has declared that frozen fruits and veggies are just as nutritious as fresh. Some say they may even be *more* nutritious, because they are usually frozen immediately after harvesting—whereas fresh produce may sit around the grocery store for days or even weeks. It's also just incredibly convenient to have a stash of frozen foods in your freezer, available for use on a moment's notice. And we all know that a Lazy Gourmet loves convenience.

HOW TO HEAT OIL (OR BUTTER)

Numerous recipes begin, "Heat oil in a skillet until hot but not smoking," but you might wonder how you're supposed to know if it is hot enough. With butter, it's fairly easy to tell, since it becomes liquid and you can see it bubbling away. It's a little trickier with oil, but only a little. One way to tell if oil is hot is that it will begin to shimmer. If you're still not sure if it is hot enough, throw a small piece of whatever you are cooking into it. If the food immediately sizzles, you know your oil is hot. If it doesn't sizzle, remove the bit of food and wait another minute or two.

HOW TO COOK PASTA

Set a big pot of water (enough to allow the pasta plenty of room to circulate as it cooks) over high heat. Toss in several healthy pinches of salt. (Adding salt is crucial for giving flavor to the noodles themselves. Salting them after cooking or salting the sauce will not prevent the noodles themselves from being bland.) Bring water to a boil and add pasta. Lower heat just enough to prevent water from boiling over, and cook, stirring occasionally to keep pasta from sticking together or to the bottom of the pot. Consult the pasta package for recommended cooking time, generally somewhere between 8 and 12 minutes. Taste a piece—if it's too hard to bite, let it cook a little longer. Pasta is done when it's chewy and tender, but still a little firm in the center. (This state is called *al dente*, meaning "to the teeth" in Italian—referring to the pasta's chewable firmness. Overcooked pasta becomes soft and bloated.) If you are making a warm dish, reserve about 1 cup pasta cooking water in case you need it for the sauce. (This water, unlike water straight from the tap, will add a bit of flavor to your sauce and will also help to thicken a sauce since it contains starch from the pasta.) Drain pasta in a colander set over the sink. If you're making a cold pasta salad, rinse the pasta with cold water to hasten cooling and to wash off any excess starch. If you're making a warm dish, don't rinse it.

For sauced pasta dishes, you may want to cook the pasta until it is just slightly underdone and finish cooking it in the sauce. This will both help to thicken your sauce and help your pasta really absorb the flavors of the sauce.

SALT DOESN'T JUST ADD SALTINESS

One of your authors (if you read the introduction to this book you can guess which one) learned this rule late in life. After a couple of frustrating bouts with dull, bland home fries, she had a lightbulb moment when she discovered a key rule of cooking: salt doesn't just make stuff salty; it's more like a magical ingredient that functions in a multitude of ways. As we describe on page 15, salt balances out the flavors of whatever you're cooking, making sweet, sour, or bitter flavors more prominent; tenderizes meat; and draws moisture from vegetables, which aids in caramelization. If your soup tastes bland despite the fact that it's packed with innately delicious ingredients, add a pinch of salt and—abracadabra!—taste it again. Same with stews, roasted veggies, meats, sandwiches, and even desserts. Don't overdo it—add a pinch at a time and taste as you go. Read more about salt on page 15.

HOW TO COOK MEAT

There are four important rules to remember when cooking meat on the stovetop—whether it's chicken, beef, pork, lamb, or even fish.

1. Make sure the pan is very hot before you add the meat. (The meat should cause a boisterous sizzle the instant it hits the pan.)
2. Leave the meat alone until it's time to flip it. Meat will naturally release from the pan when the first side is properly seared. If you pull it off before then, you'll leave the beautiful and delicious caramelized crust on the pan.
3. Don't press down on the meat while it is cooking. We know you like to hear the juices sizzle when they hit the pan, but you want that juice to stay in your meat and make it, well, juicy!
4. Always let meat rest for at least 5 minutes or so before slicing it so that it reabsorbs its juices and stays tender. Trust us, if you don't, you will have dry meat. And no one wants to eat dry meat.

AVOID STICKY SITUATIONS

Don't you hate it when you measure something sticky like honey and half of it sticks to the measuring cup? Try oiling your measuring cup with vegetable or olive oil spray before measuring and even the stickiest ingredients will slide right out.

PURÉE AWAY YOUR CARES

When you're making a soup or sauce that will ultimately be puréed, you can be super lax about how you cut the ingredients that will go into it. With chunky vegetables like carrots or potatoes, you want to make sure the pieces are roughly the same size so that they cook evenly, but they don't have to look pretty. Fresh herbs like cilantro or mint can be thrown in stem and all. (Herbs with woodier stems like rosemary or thyme still need to be destemmed first.)

FORGOT TO SOFTEN YOUR BUTTER?

Not to worry: use this simple trick to soften butter in a flash. Slice the stick lengthwise into four ½-inch-thick pieces and lay them side by side on a piece of waxed or parchment paper. Lay another piece of waxed or parchment paper on top and roll with a rolling pin to about ¼ inch or ⅛ inch thick. Voilà—soft butter!

GET THE MOST ZESTINESS FROM YOUR CITRUS

When a recipe calls for both the zest and juice of a citrus fruit, zest it first (ideally, directly into the other ingredients so you get all of the intensely flavored oil) and then juice it.

ASK YOUR BUTCHER TO DO YOUR WORK FOR YOU

Cutting beef into bite-sized pieces, boning chicken, or trimming the fat from a roast can really suck up a lot of time—especially if you don't have great knives and a degree in butchery. The good news for Lazy Gourmets is that most butchers will happily do your prep for you—they've got all the right tools and they know how to handle a piece of meat. They'll remove bones, trim fat, take off unwanted skin—even dice it or slice it into perfect stir-fry-sized pieces. For best results, try to time your shopping for the least busy times of day, be friendly, and ask nicely.

KEEP YOUR KNIVES SHARP

Sharp knives make prep easier, faster, and, perhaps surprisingly, safer. Have your knives professionally sharpened about once every year and use your honer (that long, cylindrical piece of steel that comes with many knife sets) often to keep the blades straight in the meantime.

TRIMMING ASPARAGUS

Recipes that include asparagus always instruct the reader to trim off the ends before cooking. That's because the ends are too hard and woody to eat. But how do you know where the boundary is between the inedible and the delectable? Hold the spear in both hands, gently bending it a couple of inches up from the end. The spear will break naturally at the boundary, leaving you with perfectly palatable asparagus. If presentation is important, you can trim the broken ends with a knife to tidy them up.

MAKE LEFTOVERS EASY TO USE

Don't you hate it when a recipe calls for half a can of coconut milk, two tablespoons of tomato paste, or two chipotle chiles out of a can of *chipotles en adobo*? What, you wonder, are you supposed to do with the rest? Spoon them into ice cube trays, freeze overnight, and pop them out and store them in freezer storage bags (clearly marked, of course) in your freezer for months. The next time you need a small amount, simply pop out a cube or four and drop it right into whatever you are cooking.

MAKE MEAT SLICING EASIER

Slicing raw meat neatly into thin strips can be challenging. Try freezing your meat for 30 minutes prior to slicing and it will be much easier.

EGG SEPARATING MADE EASY

Break eggs into a funnel set over a cup—the white will flow through the hole while the yolk will remain happily nestled inside the funnel!

KEEP YOUR APPLIANCES WITHIN REACH

If you're lucky enough to have plenty of counter or shelf space, we recommend keeping your food processor, blender, and other cooking appliances in plain view and well within reach. When appliances are hidden away in a high-up cupboard or stored out in the garage, it will always seem like a huge hassle to retrieve and use them. If they're as easy to access as your toaster, you'll use them without giving it a second thought—saving you from the drudgery of chopping, mincing, and mixing by hand.

CHOPPING, SLICING, DICING, AND MORE

Ever wondered why there are so many different words for cutting up food? If you don't know a slice from a dice, here's a quick primer that will help you keep them all straight.

CHOP: Cut into bite-sized pieces, 1 inch or smaller.
CUBE: Cut into a uniform cube shape, around ½ inch.
DICE: Cut into very small cubes, around ⅛ inch to ¼ inch.
MINCE: Cut into very small pieces, smaller than ⅛ inch.
SLICE: Cut into thin, flat pieces.
SHRED: Cut into small, narrow strips, usually with the large holes of a grater or a food processor fitted with a shredding disc. Cooked meat is also often "shredded" using either your hands or two forks to pull it apart.
GRATE: Reduce to very thin shreds, usually with the small holes of a grater, a Microplane grater, or a food processor fitted with a grating disc.
JULIENNE: Cut into matchstick-sized strips, around ⅛ inch thick by 2 inches long.
CHIFFONADE: This French term (literally, "made from rags") refers to a preparation of leafy vegetables or herbs by cutting them into fine strips or shreds (for example, "basil

chiffonade"). To cut a chiffonade, make a little stack of like-sized leaves, roll them up tightly, and then slice the roll to create little bundles of ribbons.

POTS AND PANS

There are many different kinds of cooking vessels and dishes, each with its own properties and purpose. Here are a few of the most common.

POT: A deep, round container that usually has two handles and a lid.

SKILLET OR FRYING PAN: A low pan with one handle and short, outward-flaring sides. They are used for cooking foods over high heat, so they should be thick, sturdy, and conduct heat evenly. They're typically around 8 to 12 inches in diameter.

SAUTÉ PAN: A frying pan with vertical (nonsloping) sides.

SAUCEPAN: A deep pan with one long handle and straight or flared sides that are usually at least 3 inches high. A saucepan often includes a tight-fitting cover. Saucepans are made from various materials including aluminum, anodized aluminum, ceramic, copper, enameled cast iron or steel, glass, or stainless steel.

STOCKPOT: A large—anywhere from 6 quarts to 20 quarts—round container that usually has two handles and a lid. Stockpots are used for making stocks and soups, but they are also often used for making sauces, stews, or braised meat dishes. When we call for a stockpot in our recipes, one on the smaller end of the scale—say, 6 or 8 quarts—will do.

DUTCH OVEN: A heavy, deep pot with a heavy lid, typically made from cast iron, and used for cooking dishes that benefit from slow cooking over a low heat.

BAKING DISH: A dish with sides a couple of inches high, of varying shapes and sizes, used in the oven. They are typically made of stoneware, cast iron, enameled cast iron, or glass.

BAKING SHEET: A flat, rectangular metal pan used in the oven or broiler and typically used for baking flat, nonjuicy items like cookies.

NONREACTIVE PANS

Sometimes you'll read a recipe that specifically calls for a nonreactive pan. This is a nonporous pan that does not produce a chemical reaction when it comes into contact with acidic foods like vinegar. Aluminum, copper, and cast iron are reactive, while stainless steel, anodized aluminum, glass, clay, and enamel are not.

Chapter Three

THE LAZY GOURMET TOOLKIT

Don't worry, you don't need a professionally equipped kitchen to be a Lazy Gourmet. In fact, having spent many years cooking in cramped, ill-equipped San Francisco apartment kitchens, we're living proof that you can get by with the most rudimentary of culinary setups. That said, there are a handful of tools that we believe will make your cooking—dare we say your life—both lazier *and* more gourmet.

CERAMIC RAMEKINS

"Let's put it in a ramekin!" We say it so often it's practically our official motto. But over and over again we prove to ourselves that just about anything seems more sophisticated when it's baked and served in individual portions in cute little pots. A soufflé is lovely, but personal mini soufflés, served hot right from the oven to your guests' plates, will have them marveling at your style and mastery. Ramekins come in a range of sizes, but for your first purchase we suggest buying a set of six 8-ouncers. If you shop carefully you can find them for a couple of dollars apiece—it's a small investment that will more than pay for itself in dividends of diner appreciation.

COOKING TIMER

Don't risk it. The $5 or $10 you shell out on a good timer will prevent you from ever again having to scrub a scorched skillet or dump an incinerated entrée straight into the trash. If you've never lost yourself in a fine bottle of wine and a riveting "Stars Who Have Cellulite" exposé only to be jolted out of your euphoria by the smell of a forgotten dinner turned to ashes, consider yourself lucky. But as any cardplayer knows, luck never lasts for long.

IMMERSION BLENDER (AKA HAND-HELD BLENDER)

Dazzling color and satisfying flavor make homemade soups one of the surest ways to impress dinner guests. A hand blender lets you purée your soup right in the pot—no waiting for it to cool down, no transferring in small batches, no dirtying extra dishes. You can also use your hand blender to make milkshakes and smoothies right in your glass.

GARLIC PRESS

Mincing garlic cloves with a knife can be tedious and dangerous for novice fingers. A simple, handheld garlic press makes this frequent task a snap by squishing the cloves through a small grid of holes like a Play-Doh machine. Some non-Lazy Gourmets are vocal opponents of the garlic press, claiming it changes the garlic's flavor, but unless you can detect the difference yourself we suggest you save your fingers and your time and press away.

MICROPLANE® GRATER

A hand-held flat grater, like those originally invented by Microplane, makes grating cheese a breeze. It's also the best tool we've found for zesting citrus fruits. A basic Microplane grater resembles a woodworker's rasp and, in fact, was originally designed by its inventors as a newer, sharper woodworking tool. Their manufacturing process creates extra-sharp teeth—great for filing wood, but also a huge help in the kitchen. In addition to cheese and zest, spices like nutmeg can be grated with a Microplane grater.

FOOD PROCESSOR

This is probably the most controversial kitchen tool here in Lazy Gourmet Land. We won't name names, but one of us swears by her food processor, lazily choosing the quick press of a button over manual chopping, while the other banishes hers to the dark depths of her tallest cabinet, lazily choosing manual chopping over washing appliances. Whether you're a lover or a hater, the food processor undeniably speeds food prep—chopping, puréeing, shredding, and grinding foods in seconds flat. It's the retrieval and cleanup that give rise to debate. Yes, it takes a little extra time to pull it out (if you keep it hidden away, that is) and wash (though most are dishwasher safe), but give it an honored position in plain view in your kitchen and you just may find it makes your cooking loads easier.

HIGH-QUALITY KNIVES

High-quality knives are sharper and maintain their cutting edge longer than their cheap counterparts, and sharp knives make cutting food easier (and safer!). Do yourself a favor and invest in a few good knives. We recommend a good-sized (6-inch or 8-inch) chef's knife, a small paring knife, and a proper bread knife at the very least. If you've got extra cash burning a hole in your pocket, treat yourself to a delightfully sleek and sharp santoku knife and a good carving knife as well. When blades begin to dull, spring for a professional sharpening.

KITCHEN SHEARS

These super-sharp all-purpose kitchen scissors come in handy for everything from snipping herbs to dicing chicken to opening packages. Look for a pair that comes apart into two pieces so that you can get into the crevices for thorough cleaning.

Part 2:
The Recipes

Chapter Four

SNACKS AND STARTERS

Basil Leaf and Goat Cheese Wraps

This simple, beautiful appetizer is not only unbelievably delicious, it's also an engaging conversation piece. Just set out the ingredients and your guests will be so intrigued and delighted that they won't even realize you're making them do all the work.

> 30–40 big, fresh-looking basil leaves
> 5 ounces chèvre
> 1 dry pint (30–40) cherry tomatoes
> ½ cup toasted pine nuts

Place basil leaves on a serving platter. Serve the cheese, tomatoes, and pine nuts in small serving dishes, with a spreading knife for the cheese and a small spoon for the pine nuts. Direct diners to take a basil leaf and wrap it around some cheese, a tomato, and a couple of pine nuts.

Makes 30 to 40 wraps.

Orange-Spiced Pecans

More addictive than crack, these spicy-sweet morsels are always a hit. Put them in a fancy jar and give them as a hostess gift, and you're sure to be invited back.

olive or vegetable oil or spray
2 tablespoons unsalted butter
1 tablespoon sugar
grated zest of 1 medium orange
¼–½ teaspoon cayenne pepper
1 teaspoon kosher salt
1½ cups pecan halves

Lay a large piece of aluminum foil or parchment paper on a counter and coat lightly with olive or vegetable oil. In a small saucepan, melt the butter over medium heat. When butter begins to bubble, add sugar, zest, cayenne, and salt. Stir until sugar and salt dissolve and zest is well distributed in the mixture. Add nuts and cook, stirring, 3 minutes more. Transfer nuts to foil or parchment and spread in a single layer. Allow to cool to room temperature.

Makes about 1½ cups.

Make it ahead

The pecans can be stored in an airtight container on the countertop for a few days.

Serve it with

✦ Olives and assorted cheeses as part of an appetizer platter

✦ Pear, Escarole, and Blue Cheese Salad (page 57) or any salad of mixed greens with vinaigrette and fruit

Change it up

✦ For an Indian-flavored version, substitute a couple of teaspoons of curry powder for the orange zest.

Spicy Pickled Carrots

San Francisco's famous Tartine restaurant serves its mouthwatering sandwiches with a precious little garnish of pickled carrots. After years of fantasizing about plunging our greedy fists right into that big glass carrot jar on the counter, we realized we could just make our own! This is not Tartine's recipe (as far as we know), but it sure is good. Enjoy as a party appetizer, as a snack, or tossed into green salads.

1½ pounds carrots, peeled and cut into sticks
1½ cups cider vinegar
1½ cups water
⅓ cup sugar
2–4 medium jalapeño chiles, stemmed and quartered lengthwise (seeds included)
2 tablespoons dill seeds
2 teaspoons caraway seeds
2 tablespoons kosher salt

Bring a nonreactive saucepan (page 25) of water to a boil over high heat. Drop carrots into boiling water and cook for 1 minute, to blanch. Drain in a colander and transfer to a bowl. Combine vinegar, water, sugar, chiles, dill seeds, caraway seeds, and salt in the saucepan and bring to a boil. Reduce heat and simmer 2 to 3 minutes. Pour vinegar mixture over carrots and let cool for about an hour. For maximum flavor, let carrots sit in the fridge for a day before serving.

Make it ahead

The pickled carrots can be stored in a jar in the fridge for about a month.

Serve it with

✦ Herbed Tuna Salad Sandwiches (page 86), Portobello Mushroom Sandwiches (page 84), or any sandwich or burger

Change it up

✦ Try adding cloves, peppercorns, mustard seeds, cinnamon sticks, or sliced garlic to the vinegar mixture.
✦ Substitute 1 to 2 tablespoons crushed red pepper for the jalapeños.
✦ This recipe also works beautifully for green beans, cauliflower, turnips, radishes, and asparagus.

Spicy Szechuan-Style Pickled Vegetables

These spicy pickles have a distinctly Chinese flavor, owing to the use of Szechuan peppercorns. Unrelated to the more familiar black peppercorns we keep on our tables, Szechuan peppercorns have an unusual earthy-spicy-floral flavor.

3 medium carrots, peeled and sliced into ¼-inch-thick rounds
3 medium turnips, halved or quartered and sliced ¼ inch thick
1 bunch radishes, stems removed, halved lengthwise
½ small head of green cabbage, core removed, leaves sliced into ½-inch-thick wedges
3½ cups unseasoned rice vinegar
2½ cups water
¼ cup kosher salt
4–6 red jalapeño chiles, stemmed, halved lengthwise, seeded, and sliced
3-inch piece fresh ginger, peeled and sliced ½ inch thick
2 tablespoons Szechuan peppercorns
4–6 whole dried hot red chiles (optional)

Bring a stockpot of water to a boil over high heat. Drop carrots, turnips, radishes, and cabbage wedges into boiling water and cook 1 minute, to blanch. Drain and place in a large bowl or storage container. In a nonreactive saucepan (page 25), combine vinegar, water, salt, fresh chiles, ginger, peppercorns, and dried chiles (if using), and bring to a boil. Reduce heat and simmer 2 minutes. Pour vinegar mixture over vegetables and let cool on the countertop for about an hour. Cover and refrigerate at least a day. Before serving, remove the ginger slices and dried chiles. Serve cold or at room temperature.

Make it ahead

Spicy Szechuan-Style Pickled Vegetables can be stored in an airtight container in the fridge for about a month.

Serve it with

✦ Asian-style barbecued chicken or our Five-Spice Roast Pork (page 126)

Change it up

✦ If you can't find Szechuan peppercorns, substitute half pink peppercorns and half regular black peppercorns coarsely crushed by placing them in a plastic bag and whacking them with a heavy skillet or a mallet. If you can't find pink peppercorns, feel free to use all black peppercorns, but the pickles won't have the same exotic flavor.

✦ Substitute any combination of vegetables for the turnips, carrots, radishes, and cabbage. Try small pickling cucumbers or Japanese daikon radish, for instance.

Warm Spicy Olives with Almonds and Kumquats

One surefire way to impress your guests is to use uncommon ingredients in unexpected ways. Here kumquats add sweetness, tang, and an element of surprise to a dish of almonds and olives. If you can't find kumquats, you can substitute large strips of orange zest. (Use a vegetable peeler to peel off long strips, leaving the white pith behind.)

1 tablespoon olive oil
5 kumquats, thinly sliced (seeds and ends discarded) or 5 large strips of zest from one large orange
¼–½ teaspoon crushed red pepper
2–3 whole sprigs fresh thyme
¼ teaspoon kosher salt
½ cup whole cured black olives, such as Kalamata
½ cup toasted unsalted almonds

In a medium saucepan, heat olive oil over medium heat until hot but not smoking. Add the kumquat slices or orange zest, crushed red pepper, thyme, and salt. Reduce heat to low, and cook, stirring occasionally, about 3 minutes, until fragrant. Add the olives and almonds and cook, stirring, about 2 minutes more until olives and almonds are warm. Let sit for 10 or 15 minutes before serving. To serve, scoop the olives, almonds, and kumquat slices out of the saucepan using a slotted spoon and place in small serving bowls.

Make it ahead

The mixture can be made a day ahead and stored, covered, in the fridge. Warm in a saucepan over medium heat a few minutes before serving.

Serve it with

✦ An appetizer platter that includes good feta cheese, hummus, baba ghanoush, or White Bean Spread with Parmesan and Mint (page 47)

Savory Blue Cheese Shortbread

They look like little cookies, but these salty, nutty crunchers have a surprising savory edge that makes a perfect foil for a dollop of sweet topping. Try them with our Fig and Onion Jam (page 158) or Plum and Currant Mostarda (page 159). They're also divine all by themselves.

½ cup (1 stick) unsalted butter at room temperature
8 ounces blue cheese at room temperature
1½ cups all-purpose flour
¼ teaspoon table salt
½ cup finely chopped pecans or walnuts

In the bowl of a food processor or stand mixer, or in a large bowl using a hand-held electric mixer, cream together the butter and cheese until smooth. (Alternatively, you can do the mixing by hand, using your fingers to work ingredients together.) Add flour and salt and mix until well combined. Add nuts and mix until the mixture comes together in a ball. If the mixture is crumbly, add cold water, 1 teaspoon at a time, until the dough comes together.

Spread a piece of plastic wrap on the counter and dump the dough onto it. Shape the dough into a log about 12 inches long. Wrap tightly in the plastic wrap and refrigerate a minimum of 30 minutes and up to three days.

Preheat oven to 350°F.

Using a sharp or serrated knife, slice the chilled log into thin rounds and place ¼ inch apart on a baking sheet. Bake in preheated oven for 25 to 30 minutes, until lightly browned. Remove pan from oven and let cool. Serve at room temperature.

Makes 35 to 40 crackers.

Make it ahead
The dough will keep in the fridge for several days. Baked, the crackers will keep in an airtight container on the countertop for a couple of days.

Serve it with
✦ Fig and Onion Jam (page 158)
✦ Plum and Currant Mostarda (page 159)
✦ Slow-Roasted Tomatoes (page 43)

Change it up

+ Substitute just about any cheese or nut combo that strikes your fancy—try chèvre, sharp Cheddar, or aged Gouda with almonds, pistachios, or hazelnuts.
+ A combination of Parmesan, pine nuts, and 1 tablespoon coarsely chopped rosemary, with the addition of ⅓ cup heavy cream (to compensate for the dryness of the Parmesan), is particularly delectable.
+ Try adding ¼ cup of chopped dried fruit such as raisins, dates, or dried figs with the nuts.

Manchego-Stuffed Dates

Sticky-sweet dates and hard salty cheese are a perfect match. Serve these flavorful little morsels as part of an appetizer platter with cheese, cured meats, and roasted or marinated vegetables.

18 pitted dates
4 ounces Manchego cheese

Cut cheese into small wedges and slip into the center of the dates.

Makes 18 stuffed dates.

Make it ahead

The dates can be stuffed several hours ahead and stored, covered, in the fridge. Allow to come to room temperature before serving.

Serve it with

+ Assorted cheeses, nuts, and cured meats, such as prosciutto, as part of an appetizer spread
+ A mixed green salad dressed with Sherry-Shallot Vinaigrette (page 150)

Change it up

+ Substitute any strongly flavored, salty cheese for the Manchego. Try a good imported Parmesan or Roquefort.
+ Drizzle with chile oil just before serving for a spicy kick.

Cheese Crisps

These pretty little pastries make a festive appetizer on their own, or use them as a fancy garnish for soups or salads. Be sure to read the section on working with frozen puff pastry (page 14).

1 sheet of frozen puff pastry, defrosted
1 ounce (about ⅓ cup) grated Parmesan cheese
2 tablespoons pine nuts
2 teaspoons minced fresh rosemary (optional)

Lay the pastry out on a work surface and sprinkle the cheese, nuts, and rosemary (if using) evenly over the top. Starting with one of the long sides, roll the pastry into a tight log. Wrap the log in plastic wrap and refrigerate at least 1 hour and up to two days.

Preheat oven to 400°F.

Lay a piece of parchment paper, large enough to cover the bottom of a baking sheet, on your work surface. Unwrap the pastry log and, using a sharp or serrated knife, cut into ½-inch-thick slices. Lay the slices on the parchment paper about 3 inches apart. Place another piece of parchment paper over the pastry slices and roll with a rolling pin until each slice is about ¼ inch thick. Slide the parchment with the pastry slices onto a baking sheet and remove the top piece of parchment. Bake in preheated oven until cheese is bubbly and pastry is golden brown, 15 to 20 minutes. Remove from oven and let cool on the pan for a few minutes before removing with a spatula. Serve warm or at room temperature.

Makes about 15 to 20 crisps.

Make it ahead
The pastry log can be assembled and kept, wrapped in plastic, for at least a couple of days in the fridge. When you're ready to cook the crisps, just slice, roll, and bake.

Serve it with
✦ Caramelized Onion Soup (page 69) or Parsnip and Apple Soup (page 77)
✦ Roasted Beet and Arugula Salad (page 59) or any salad of mixed greens with vinaigrette
✦ As an alternative to plain croutons with a classic Caesar salad

Change it up

Instead of Parmesan, pine nuts, and rosemary, try:

✦ 4 ounces crumbled blue cheese and 1 tablespoon of chopped walnuts

✦ 4 ounces crumbled feta cheese and ½ to 1 teaspoon crushed red pepper

✦ ¼ cup Olive and Sun-Dried Tomato Tapenade (page 46)

✦ ¼ cup store-bought pesto and 2 tablespoons pine nuts

Endive Spoons with Apples and Aged Gouda

Stuffed endive leaves make a tasty—and beautiful—appetizer. Aged Gouda is one of our favorite cheeses—both salty and sweet, with a robust, caramel-like flavor. And tiny calcium lactate crystals that form as the cheese ages give it a delicate and tantalizing crunch. If you've never had aged Gouda before, buy a little extra so you can try some unaccompanied slices in all their self-sufficient glory.

1 medium apple (any type), cored and minced (about 1 cup)
3 ounces (about 1 cup) finely grated aged Gouda
¼ cup minced red, yellow, or white onion
½ cup finely chopped toasted pecans
2 Belgian endives
freshly ground black pepper, to taste

In a small bowl, mix apple, Gouda, onion, and pecans. Chop the stem end off each endive and separate the leaves. Spoon some of the apple mixture onto the sturdy end of each endive leaf. Arrange neatly on a serving platter and sprinkle generously with pepper.

Makes about 20 endive spoons.

Change it up

✦ Try smoked Gouda instead of aged Gouda.

✦ Substitute 3 thinly sliced green onions for the minced onion.

Rosemary-Cheddar Crostini

These savory canapés are always a hit. Why use white Cheddar and not orange? We just think a screaming neon-orange brick of cheese looks, well, yucky. That bright orange color comes from annatto, a food-grade dye made from the annatto seed. It won't hurt you, but your platter of cheese toasts will look so much more sophisticated in understated tones of muted beige.

> 1 10-ounce skinny baguette
> 5 ounces (about 1⅔ cups) shredded sharp white Cheddar cheese
> 3 tablespoons chopped fresh rosemary leaves
> kosher salt

Preheat oven to 400°F.

Cut the baguette into slices about ½ inch thick and place on a baking sheet. Top each slice with some grated cheese and a sprinkle of rosemary. Sprinkle the toasts with a couple of pinches of salt and bake in preheated oven for 10 to 12 minutes, or until lightly toasted and crunchy.

Makes about 40 crostini.

Make it ahead

Of course they're best served warm, fresh from the oven, but they'll actually keep pretty well for a couple of days in an airtight container.

Serve it with

✦ Roasted Tomato-Curry Soup (page 76) or Parsnip and Apple Soup (page 77)

Slow-Roasted Tomatoes

About 90 percent of what your authors talk and think about is the mind-blowing incredible-ness of slow-roasted tomatoes. Using what we speculate to be magic, this all-day process trans-forms normal tomatoes into something more sweet, intense, and delicious than you can possibly imagine. We recommend Romas because their meaty flesh and thin skin make them ideal for this kind of treatment, but any tomatoes can be used; you'll just need to adjust the timing depending on their size. You'll never let an unused tomato go bad again.

¼ cup olive oil
4 pounds ripe Roma tomatoes (about 15), halved, stem ends removed
1 teaspoon kosher salt

Preheat oven to 200°F.

Pour olive oil onto a large, rimmed baking sheet. Roll the tomato halves around on the baking sheet until they're coated with oil. Place them, cut side up, on the baking sheet and sprinkle them with salt. Bake tomatoes in preheated oven until they have shrunk to about one-third their original size and are soft and juicy and beginning to caramelize around the edges—6 to 8 hours. Remove baking sheet from the oven, and allow the tomatoes to cool to room temperature.

Make it ahead

If you somehow manage not to eat them all immediately, you can store them, covered, in the fridge for a couple of weeks. You can even freeze them for several months—a great tip for those of you lucky enough to have gardens that produce more summer tomatoes than you know what to do with.

Serve it with
+ Bread and cheese, as part of an appetizer spread
+ Grilled meats or seafood
+ Pasta topped with freshly grated Parmesan
+ Baked Polenta with Mascarpone and Corn (page 143)

Change it up
+ Sprinkle minced garlic on tomatoes before roasting.
+ Sprinkle herbs and spices on tomatoes before roasting; for example, ground coriander, rosemary, black pepper, basil, oregano, ground fennel, thyme, or marjoram.

Raita

Raita is a cool, refreshing Indian condiment, usually served alongside spicy dishes. It can also be served as an appetizer, with vegetables, crackers, or bread. You can find the Indian flatbread called *nan* at many supermarkets, or toss authenticity to the wind and use pita bread instead. Honestly, raita is so delicious that it hardly matters what you choose to use as your delivery vehicle! This dish gets better as the flavors meld, so it's best made a day ahead and stored, covered, in the fridge until serving time.

1 medium cucumber, peeled, seeded, and grated
1 cup plain whole-milk yogurt
½ teaspoon kosher salt
3 tablespoons minced fresh mint leaves
½ teaspoon ground cumin

Wrap grated cucumber in a paper towel or dishcloth and squeeze to remove excess moisture. In a medium bowl, combine cucumber, yogurt, salt, mint, and cumin and stir to combine. Chill at least 30 minutes before serving.

Makes about 1½ cups.

Make it ahead
Raita can be stored in the fridge, covered, for a couple of days.

Serve it with
✦ Fresh vegetables, nan, or pita chips for dipping
✦ Grilled chicken or fish, especially tandoori-style
✦ Roasted veggies rolled up in Middle Eastern flatbread for a tasty and healthy wrap

Change it up
✦ Add seeded, chopped tomatoes or very thinly sliced red onion with the cucumber.
✦ Try chopped cilantro instead of, or in addition to, the mint.

Spicy Feta Spread

A tiny bit of this flavorful delight goes a long way. Don't worry if you don't have a food processor—just mince the garlic first and mix ingredients with a fork, mashing the feta well. Spread leftovers on a sandwich with roasted veggies, or crumble into a green salad.

1 small clove garlic
6 ounces (about 1¼ cups) crumbled feta
2 tablespoons fresh oregano leaves
½–1 teaspoon crushed red pepper
2 tablespoons olive oil
3 tablespoons lemon juice (from about 1 lemon)

Chop garlic in a food processor. Add feta, oregano, crushed red pepper, olive oil, and lemon juice and process until well combined. Serve at room temperature.

Makes about 1 cup.

Make it ahead

The spread can be stored in the fridge, covered, for a couple of days. Bring to room temperature before serving.

Serve it with

✦ Toasted pita wedges, cucumber slices, and sweet cherry tomatoes

Change it up

✦ Substitute another fresh herb, such as dill, for the oregano.

✦ Use as a filling for roasted, peeled, and seeded mild or medium-spicy long peppers, such as Anaheim, Fresno, or pasilla chiles. Broil the stuffed peppers until bubbly, about 5 or 6 minutes, and serve hot with crusty bread.

Olive and Sun-Dried Tomato Tapenade

This salty, tangy olive spread is great on crusty bread or crackers, tossed with pasta, or dolloped onto grilled or poached fish. It's also the featured player in our Olive and Sun-Dried Tomato Tapenade Sandwich (page 87). A food processor makes quick work of this recipe, but you can also simply mince all the ingredients finely and stir them together in a bowl.

1 clove garlic
8 ounces pitted Kalamata olives, rinsed and drained
1 tablespoon capers, drained
4 ounces (about ½ cup) oil-packed sun-dried tomatoes, drained
2 tablespoons (tightly packed) minced fresh basil
1 teaspoon anchovy paste (optional)
zest of half a lemon
2 tablespoons lemon juice (from about half a lemon)
2 tablespoons olive oil

In the bowl of a food processor, mince the garlic. Add olives, capers, sun-dried tomatoes, and basil leaves and process to a chunky purée. Add anchovy paste (if using), lemon zest, lemon juice, and olive oil and process until just combined. (Alternatively, you can mince all ingredients by hand and stir together in a bowl.)

Makes about 1½ cups.

Make it ahead:
Tapenade will keep, covered, in the fridge for several days.

Serve it with
+ Crusty bread, pita chips, or crackers
+ Hummus, feta, and fresh vegetables, as part of an appetizer platter
+ Baked, broiled, grilled, or poached fish or seafood

Change it up
+ Replace the sun-dried tomatoes with several minced artichoke hearts or half a roasted red bell pepper.

White Bean Spread with Parmesan and Mint

Fresh garlic and mint give this deceptively simple spread intense flavor, cayenne pepper adds a nice kick, and rich Parmesan cheese pulls it all together. This is one recipe that really requires the use of a food processor. Other methods of mashing or puréeing the beans will result in an unpleasant grainy texture.

1 small clove garlic, peeled
1 14-ounce can cannellini beans, drained and rinsed
2 tablespoons olive oil
½ cup (tightly packed) fresh mint leaves
2 tablespoons water
3 tablespoons lemon juice (from about 1 lemon)
¼ teaspoon kosher salt
⅛–¼ teaspoon cayenne pepper
3 ounces (about 1 cup) grated Parmesan cheese

Chop garlic in food processor. Add beans, olive oil, mint, water, lemon juice, salt, and cayenne and purée until smooth. Add cheese and process until well combined.

Makes about 1¾ cups.

Make it ahead

The spread will keep, covered, in the fridge for a couple of days.

Serve it with

✦ Toasted baguette slices
✦ Raw radicchio, endive, or other vegetables for dipping
✦ Pita chips or crackers
✦ Baked, broiled, or grilled salmon or shrimp

Change it up

✦ Use basil in place of the mint.

Artichokes with Lemon-Tahini Dip

Artichokes add a dramatic presence to any table. Plus they're a natural choice for lazy hosts, as the guests wind up doing most of the labor! As an alternative to the Lemon-Tahini Dip, try dipping your artichoke leaves in our Balsamic Syrup (page 147) or any of our Compound Butters (page 152), melted.

4 medium artichokes
1 recipe Lemon-Tahini Dip (page 156)

Clean the artichokes under running water, brushing lightly with a vegetable brush to remove the bitter outer film if necessary. Cut off the thorny portion, about the top inch or so, from each artichoke. (A serrated knife works well.) You don't need to remove all of the thorns, since the smaller ones will soften during cooking. Trim the stem down to about an inch in length.

Place the artichokes, cut side down, in a vegetable steamer inside a large pot containing about an inch of water. Cover and bring to a boil over high heat. Reduce heat to low and simmer until stems are easily pierced with a knife, about 30 minutes for medium artichokes. Alternatively, bring a large pot of salted water to a boil, add artichokes, reduce heat to low, and simmer, covered, until stems are easily pierced with a knife, about 30 minutes for medium artichokes. Adjust time for smaller or larger artichokes.

Drain artichokes before serving by placing them upside down in a colander for a few minutes. Pluck off the tough outer leaves at the bottom of the artichoke and discard them. Serve with one big bowl or several individual dishes of Lemon-Tahini Dip.

Serves 4.

Make it ahead

The artichokes and dip can both be made ahead and stored, separately, in covered containers in the fridge for a couple of days.

Baked Brie with Dried Cranberries and Pistachios

Almost as easy as serving plain Brie right out of the wrapper, this baked version adds color and flair—not to mention scrumptious flavors. Toss some good crusty French bread slices into the oven for a few minutes while the Brie is baking, and serve together.

1 8-ounce wheel of Brie
½ cup dried cranberries
⅓ cup shelled, unsalted pistachios
1–2 tablespoons honey

Preheat oven to 350°F.

Place Brie on a decorative, rimmed, ovenproof dish. Sprinkle dried berries and pistachios over the Brie, right onto the rind, and into the dish around the Brie. Bake 10 to 15 minutes, until cheese starts to ooze out the bottom a little. Let cool for a few minutes, and then drizzle honey over the berries and nuts. Serve with a spreading knife, warning guests to beware of the hot dish.

Serves 6 to 8.

Serve it with

✦ Warm French bread or good crackers

Change it up

✦ Experiment with different kinds of dried fruits (other berries, cherries, chopped apricots, chopped dates) and nuts (almonds, pine nuts, walnuts).
✦ Replace the dried fruit and honey with jarred chutney.

Roasted Potato Slices with Chipotle-Lime Sour Cream

1½ pounds russet potatoes (about 2 medium potatoes)
olive oil or olive oil spray
1 teaspoon kosher salt, divided
1 cup (6 ounces) sour cream
1 to 2 teaspoons minced chipotle chiles from a can of *chipotles en adobo*
grated zest of 1 lime
1 tablespoon fresh lime juice (from about half a lime)
½ teaspoon ground cumin
½ teaspoon honey
⅓ cup minced cilantro leaves

Preheat oven to 500°F. Lightly oil a baking sheet.

Slice the potatoes into ⅛-inch rounds. Place in a single layer on prepared baking sheet. Brush or spray tops of potato slices with oil and sprinkle with ½ teaspoon salt. Bake 12 to 15 minutes, until potatoes are lightly crisped and golden brown. Let cool 10 minutes. Transfer to a serving platter.

While potatoes are baking, mix sour cream, remaining ½ teaspoon salt, chipotle chiles, lime zest and juice, cumin, and honey. Top each potato slice with a dollop of the sour cream mixture and a sprinkle of minced cilantro.

Makes 40 to 50 pieces.

Change it up
+ Spread a rounded teaspoon or so of mashed avocado on top of the potato before adding the sour cream.

Scallop Ceviche with Papaya and Chiles

Ceviche is a South and Central American specialty of seafood marinated in citrus juices. The citric acids alter the proteins in the fish, making its flesh opaque and firm, as if it had been cooked with heat. It isn't cooked, however, in the sense that all bacteria is destroyed, so it's important to use only perfectly fresh, carefully handled, sushi-grade scallops. Depending on the cuisine of the country, ceviche might be served with cold sweet potato slices, corn on the cob, potato chips, tortilla chips, or even popcorn.

1 pound sea scallops, rinsed, patted dry, and cut into ½-inch pieces
1 cup lime juice (from 10 to 12 limes)
½ cup diced red onion
1 large jalapeño or serrano chile, stemmed, seeded, and finely diced
½ teaspoon kosher salt
1½ cups cubed papaya
¼ cup (loosely packed) minced cilantro
1 large bag of potato chips or tortilla chips

Place scallops in a large nonreactive dish (page 25) and cover completely with lime juice. Stir in onion, chile, and salt. Cover and refrigerate until scallops turn opaque, about 4 hours, stirring at least once halfway through. Mix in papaya and cilantro. Return to the fridge for 15 to 30 minutes to let flavors meld. Pour off some of the lime juice before serving. Place potato chips or tortilla chips on a large serving platter with ceviche in a serving bowl in the middle.

Serves 4.

Change it up
✦ Try adding or substituting cucumber, red bell pepper, avocado, jicama, mango, pineapple, or canta-loupe.

Soy-Ginger Cured Salmon

Serve this Asian-style gravlax as an appetizer or as part of a brunch buffet. Let guests assemble their own little rice cracker canapés, or serve in bowls over warm sushi rice. Be sure to use only sushi-grade salmon.

> 1-pound filet of sushi-grade salmon, skin removed (ask your fish dealer to remove it, if possible)
> 2 tablespoons sake or vodka
> ½ cup soy sauce
> ½ cup (packed) brown sugar
> 1 tablespoon peeled and minced fresh ginger
> 6–8 sprigs fresh cilantro, plus more for garnish
> 3 green onions, pale green and white parts only, thinly sliced, for garnish
> 1–2 jalapeño chiles, stemmed, seeded, and minced, for garnish

Place the salmon in a baking dish large enough to hold it in one flat piece. Drizzle the sake or vodka over it. In a small bowl, stir the soy sauce, brown sugar, and ginger until well combined. (If desired, chop the ginger in a food processor, add the sugar and soy sauce, and process until well combined.) Pour mixture over salmon, lay cilantro sprigs on top, and cover with a large piece of plastic wrap, pressing the plastic directly onto the surface of the fish and any sauce in the dish. Place something flat, such as a plate or skillet, on top of the fish and place something heavy (unopened cans of beans make good weights) on top of that. Refrigerate at least two days and up to three, turning occasionally.

To serve, remove fish from marinade and, using a very sharp knife held at a 30° angle to the cutting surface, slice into broad, thin slices. Garnish with fresh cilantro, green onions, and minced chiles.

Serves 4 to 6.

Serve it with
+ Rice crackers and crème fraîche or sour cream
+ Warm sushi rice or plain steamed white or brown rice

Change it up
+ For a more European flavor, instead of sake or vodka, soy sauce, brown sugar, and cilantro, douse with 2 tablespoons gin and coat the entire surface with a dry rub made of ¼ cup kosher salt and ¼ cup sugar. Top with 4 or 5 crushed juniper berries and a handful of fresh dill sprigs and cure as above. Serve with thin slices of pumpernickel bread, crème fraîche, and chopped chives.

Crisped Salami and Mostarda Canapé

Lightly browned, crisped salami slices make a surprisingly perfect finger food—and serve as a tantalizing base for whatever you dollop on top. Here we pair salty salami with our tangy-sweet Plum and Currant Mostarda (page 159). If you're feeling too lazy to make the mostarda, simply use store-bought jam or chutney instead.

8 ounces Italian dry salami (about a 6-inch log), sliced into ⅛-inch thick rounds
½ cup Plum and Currant Mostarda (page 159)
½ small head of radicchio, cut into 1-inch wedges

Preheat oven to 350°F.

Place salami in a single layer on a baking sheet and bake in preheated oven until slices are lightly browned, 15 to 20 minutes. Set cooked salami on a paper towel to absorb the excess oil, and gently pat tops dry as well. Arrange slices on a serving platter and top each with a dollop of mostarda, followed by a wedge of radicchio.

Makes 25 to 30 canapés.

Make it ahead

The salami can be baked a few hours ahead and kept on the counter in an airtight container. Top with mostarda and radicchio just before serving.

Magical Asiago-Fig Bread

This bread is magical because it takes less than 15 minutes of active time to make, but we guarantee that your friends will be seriously impressed when you present them with these crusty loaves fresh from your own home oven. No-knead breads have had quite a heyday recently thanks to folks like NYC baker Jim Lahey, whose wonderful book *My Bread* first inspired us to experiment with no-knead methods. Our method is slightly different from Lahey's, but still shockingly easy and virtually foolproof. For best results, be sure to use bread flour rather than all-purpose, whole wheat, or other flours. This version using figs and cheese is one of our favorites, but the possibilities for experimentation are nearly limitless. You can also leave out the special ingredients and just make a delicious, basic loaf of bread. Be forewarned that while the recipe involves minimal hands-on cooking time, it takes anywhere from 14 to 27 hours from start to finish, so plan accordingly.

1⅓ cups cool water (from the tap is fine)
¾ teaspoon active dry yeast
½ teaspoon sugar
3 cups bread flour, plus additional flour (all-purpose is fine) for dusting
1 teaspoon table salt
6 ounces (about 1 cup) dried figs, stemmed and cut into ¼-inch dice
6 ounces Asiago cheese, cut into ¼-inch dice
2 tablespoons olive oil

Place the water in a small bowl, or better yet, a 2-cup liquid measuring cup, and sprinkle the yeast and sugar over the top. Set aside for 5 to 10 minutes.

Meanwhile, measure the bread flour into a large bowl. Add the salt and stir a bit to combine. Add the diced figs to the flour mixture and toss to combine, making sure to break up the fig pieces so they don't stick together in clumps. Add the cheese and toss again to combine.

Give the yeast mixture a stir and pour it into the flour. Using a wooden spoon at first, and then your hands, mix until the flour is incorporated, about 30 seconds. The dough should come together into a slightly sticky ball. If it's too dry to hold together, add water 1 tablespoon at a time, kneading after each addition, just until the dough comes together. Cover the bowl with a clean dishtowel and let rest, undisturbed, on your countertop for anywhere from 12 to 24 hours (the longer the better). At the end of this time, the dough will have grown significantly in size and the top will be somewhat dry and crusty.

Place a clean dishtowel on your countertop and dust lightly with flour. Turn the dough out of the bowl onto the floured towel, using a rubber spatula, if needed, to detach it from the bottom of the bowl. Fold the crusty parts of the dough inside, forming the dough back into a flattish, round shape. Wrap the towel loosely around the dough and let sit, undisturbed, on the countertop for another 1½ to 2 hours.

About 20 or 30 minutes before the end of the second rise, preheat oven to 475ºF. Brush a large baking sheet lightly with olive oil.

Turn the dough out onto a lightly floured board and divide into several equal-sized pieces—you could do 12 breadsticks or 4 mini baguettes, for instance. Form the dough pieces into whatever shape you prefer by rolling them between your hands and gently stretching them. Place the loaves on the pan, brush with a bit of olive oil, and bake in the preheated oven for 15 to 30 minutes, depending on the size of your loaves. When it's finished, the bread should be a nice golden brown on the outside. Remove from oven and let cool at least 15 minutes before slicing.

Make it ahead

Follow the instructions through the first rise of the dough and then wrap dough in plastic wrap and keep in the fridge up to several days. Remove from fridge about 2 hours before you plan to bake it, and follow the instructions for prepping the dough for the second rise. Baked, the bread will keep in the freezer for several months. Simply set it on the countertop for several hours to defrost.

Serve it with

✦ A salad of mixed greens with sherry vinaigrette, or as part of a fruit and cheese platter

Change it up

✦ Substitute any combination of cheese and dried fruit for the Asiago and figs. Try sharp white Cheddar and dried cherries, aged Gouda and dried apples, or blue cheese and dried apricots.

✦ For added crunch, add chopped pecans, walnuts, pine nuts, or almonds.

✦ For additional flavor, try adding chopped fresh herbs such as rosemary or thyme.

✦ For a more savory version, try substituting chopped olives or sun-dried tomatoes for the fruit.

Chapter Five

SALADS

Pear, Escarole, and Blue Cheese Salad

This simple salad packs all kinds of flavor; the sweet pears, mildly bitter escarole, sharp blue cheese, and rich pecans blend well with our Sherry-Shallot Vinaigrette. If you can't find escarole, substitute another slightly bitter green like arugula—or even a milder green like butter lettuce.

> 2 ripe pears, any type
> 1 1-pound head escarole, torn into pieces (about 8 cups, loosely packed)
> 3 ounces (about ½ cup) crumbled blue cheese
> 1 cup toasted pecans
> Sherry-Shallot Vinaigrette (page 150)

Quarter and core the pears and slice lengthwise into thin slices. In a large serving bowl, toss the escarole, cheese, and pecans and add vinaigrette to taste. You can toss the pears in with the salad and let guests serve themselves, or plate the salad individually, placing pear slices decoratively on top of each serving.

Serves 4.

Change it up

- ✦ Substitute feta or another cheese for the blue.
- ✦ Use Orange-Spiced Pecans (page 34) or store-bought candied pecans in place of the plain toasted nuts.

Raw Asparagus and Mâche Salad with Citrus Vinaigrette

Our friend Anthony Tassinello, an accomplished chef and the complete antithesis of a Lazy Gourmet (he built a wood-fired oven in his backyard with his own two hands just so he could make great pizzas at home. Enough said, right?), gave us the idea for this refreshing use of asparagus. It is delicious and, in fact, incredibly easy to make. Even for us regular people.

grated zest and coarsely chopped flesh of 1 Meyer lemon
¼ cup Meyer lemon juice (from about 2 Meyer lemons)
1 teaspoon Dijon mustard
1 teaspoon kosher salt
¼ cup olive oil
¾ pound asparagus, woody ends snapped off
4 cups mâche (or baby arugula if mâche is unavailable)
freshly ground black pepper to taste
1–2 ounces Parmesan cheese

In a small bowl or a jar with a tight-fitting lid, combine the lemon zest, lemon flesh, lemon juice, mustard, and salt. Add the olive oil and whisk or shake vigorously until well combined.

Slice asparagus spears on the diagonal very thin (about 1/16 inch). In a large serving bowl, toss the sliced asparagus with the dressing and set aside. While the asparagus marinates briefly in the vinaigrette, trim the root ends off the mâche, add the mâche to the dressing and asparagus, and toss gently until the leaves are evenly coated. Season with freshly ground black pepper, to taste, and shave cheese over the top using a vegetable peeler. Serve immediately.

Serves 4.

Roasted Beet and Arugula Salad

This salad is so beautiful that the fact that it also tastes amazing seems like just an added bonus. The green arugula, red beets, and stark white feta make a truly striking combination that gets any meal off to an impressive start. The beets take a while to bake and then cool, so plan accordingly. You can even roast the beets a couple of days in advance and then just assemble the salad in a matter of minutes, right before serving.

3 medium beets
6 cups (loosely packed) arugula
½ cup toasted unsalted, shelled pistachio nuts
3 ounces (about ½ cup) crumbled feta cheese
2 tablespoons chopped fresh oregano
Lemon Vinaigrette (page 148)

Preheat oven to 475°F.

Scrub beets and wrap in aluminum foil. Bake until tender and easily pierced with the tip of a sharp knife, about 75 minutes or more, depending on their size. Remove from oven and set aside to cool. When cool enough to handle, the skins should slip off easily. If not, use a sharp knife or vegetable peeler to remove skin. Slice beets into rounds, wedges, or small cubes.

In a large bowl, toss the arugula with the vinaigrette, using just enough of the vinaigrette to lightly coat the leaves.

Place a bed of the dressed arugula on a large serving platter or on individual plates. Arrange the beets on top of the arugula and drizzle a little more of the vinaigrette over them. Sprinkle crumbled feta, nuts, and oregano over the beets. Serve immediately.

Serves 4 to 6.

Make it ahead

The roasted beets can be made a couple of days ahead and stored, covered, in the fridge.

Salad of Bitter Greens with Asiago

The sweetness of our balsamic vinaigrette plays perfectly against the bitterness of the greens.

2 medium Belgian endives, halved lengthwise and thinly sliced crosswise
3 cups (loosely packed) arugula leaves
1 medium head radicchio, chopped
1 medium bunch frisée, chopped
Balsamic Vinaigrette (page 149)
4 ounces (about 1⅓ cups) grated Asiago cheese

In a large serving bowl, toss the endives, arugula, radicchio, and frisée. Dress to taste with vinaigrette. Toss cheese in gently, and serve immediately.

Serves 4 to 6.

Change it up

✦ Toss in ¼ cup of toasted pine nuts.

Raw Mushroom Salad

This simple salad is complex enough to leave as is, but it's also basic enough to permit a bit of creativity. You can toss in almost any vegetable, leafy green, or nut to customize it to your preference. See our suggestions, below, for inspiration.

1 pound crimini or button mushrooms, halved or quartered depending on their size
Lemon Vinaigrette (page 148)
3 ounces (about 1 cup) grated Parmesan cheese
1 tablespoon minced fresh tarragon

In a medium serving bowl, toss mushrooms with vinaigrette, to taste. Add cheese and tarragon and toss gently to combine. Serve immediately.

Serves 2 to 4.

Change it up
Add any of the following:
+ Thinly sliced fennel
+ Steamed asparagus, sliced on the diagonal
+ Fresh, chopped spinach leaves
+ Toasted pine nuts
+ Homemade Croutons (page 163)

Heirloom Tomato Salad with Feta, Chives, and Pine Nuts

These days, most of the fruits and vegetables you find in the supermarket have been hybridized—bred for particular qualities such as size, shape, and color. In the process, much of the true flavor is lost in exchange for uniform eye appeal. Heirloom tomatoes are tomatoes that have not been genetically engineered, so they retain all the delicious natural tomato flavor. They can be kind of funny looking—misshapen and oddly colored—but once you slice them up and place them on a platter, the array of hues is stunning.

> 2 pounds heirloom tomatoes in a variety of colors (or any good-quality tomatoes), sliced
> Balsamic Vinaigrette (page 149)
> 3 ounces (about ½ cup) crumbled feta cheese
> ⅓ cup toasted pine nuts
> 2 tablespoons chopped fresh chives

Arrange tomato slices on a large serving platter or on individual salad plates. Drizzle vinaigrette over the tomatoes to taste. Sprinkle feta, toasted pine nuts, and chopped chives on top.

Serves 4–6.

Serve it with
- ✦ Roasted Salmon with Garlic Confit (page 107)
- ✦ Top Sirloin with Charmoula on a Bed of Arugula (page 113)

Artichoke and Endive Panzanella

Panzanella is an Italian bread salad traditionally made with tomatoes. This lemony version will delight your guests with unexpected ingredients. Bonus: it's a great way to use up stale bread! If you don't have stale bread handy, just pop your bread cubes into a hot oven for a few minutes to toast them lightly. This salad is best after it sits for a few hours, allowing the bread and other ingredients to soak up the delicious dressing, so plan ahead.

3 cups cubed crusty bread, lightly toasted
1 14-ounce can artichokes in water, drained and cut into quarters
3 Belgian endives, halved lengthwise and thinly sliced crosswise
3 ounces (about 1 cup) grated Parmesan cheese
¼ cup (loosely packed) julienned fresh basil
1 recipe Lemon Vinaigrette (page 148)

In a medium salad bowl, combine the bread, artichokes, endives, cheese, and basil. Add the vinaigrette and toss until well combined. Cover and let sit in the fridge at least 30 minutes and up to several hours.

Serves 4 to 6.

Make it ahead

This salad is best made at least several hours ahead.

Serve it with

✦ An antipasto platter of aged cheeses, cured meats, and assorted olives
✦ Roasted Tomato-Curry Soup (page 76)

Change it up

✦ Add a large seeded and diced tomato just before serving for extra color and flavor.
✦ Use mint or cilantro in place of the basil.

Avocado, Jicama, and Apple Salad

The red onion and hot peppers give this sweet, refreshing salad a dose of unexpected vigor. It's perfect for an outdoor meal on a warm day, but you can also serve it indoors on a cold day, or in a grass hut on a fair day, or even in a pup tent out in the rain. We don't care. Just try it. You'll like it.

2 tablespoons lime juice (juice of 1–2 limes)
2 tablespoons olive oil
½ teaspoon kosher salt
¼–½ teaspoon freshly ground black pepper
½ teaspoon ground cumin
2 teaspoons honey
2 firm, ripe Hass avocados (the kind with bumpy black skin), peeled and diced
½ pound jicama, peeled and diced (about 1½ cups)
1 large apple (Fuji, Gala, or any other firm, sweet type), cored and diced (about 1½ cups)
¼ cup finely diced red onion
1–2 jalapeño or serrano chiles, stemmed, seeded, and finely diced

In a large serving bowl, whisk together the lime juice, olive oil, salt, pepper, cumin, and honey. Add the avocadoes, jicama, apple, onion, and chiles and stir gently to coat with the dressing. Let sit for 15 minutes to allow flavors to blend. Taste, and adjust seasoning if necessary.

Serves 4 to 6.

Serve it with
✦ Grilled chicken or fish

Change it up
✦ Substitute mango, papaya, or orange for the apple.

Watermelon, Feta, and Mint Salad

Sweet, juicy watermelon, salty feta cheese, sprightly fresh mint, and pickled red onions make for a delightfully surprising salad. Serve this refreshing treat at the height of summer when watermelons are at their sweetest. The watermelon will give off a lot of liquid after it is combined with the other ingredients, so this salad should be served immediately when all of the parts have been assembled.

¼ medium red onion, thinly sliced
½ teaspoon kosher salt
½ cup lime juice (from about 4 limes)
4 cups peeled, cubed, and seeded watermelon
2 teaspoons red wine vinegar
¼ cup minced fresh mint
3 ounces (about ½ cup) feta cheese, crumbled

Place the sliced onion in a small bowl and sprinkle with salt. Squeeze the lime juice over and add the vinegar. Stir to combine and set aside until ready to assemble salad, at least 15 minutes, preferably 30.

In a medium bowl, toss watermelon with the onion and its soaking liquid. Add mint and toss again to combine. Add feta and gently toss to distribute cheese. Serve immediately.

Serves 4.

Serve it with
✦ Spicy barbecued chicken

Fig, Mint, and Pistachio Salad

Inspired by cookbook author Viana LaPlace, this salad perfectly sums up the theme of this book: it's incredibly simple, surprisingly delicious, and certain to impress.

3 tablespoons lemon juice (from about 1 lemon)
1 tablespoon honey
½ teaspoon kosher salt
¼–½ teaspoon freshly ground black pepper
2 tablespoons olive oil
24 medium black mission figs, stemmed and quartered
⅓ cup toasted unsalted, shelled pistachio nuts
⅓ cup (tightly packed) minced fresh mint leaves

In a large serving bowl, whisk together the lemon juice, honey, salt, pepper, and olive oil. Add figs and toss gently to coat thoroughly with the dressing. Add pistachio nuts and chopped mint and toss gently until just combined.

Serves 4 to 6.

Make it ahead
    The dressing can be made a day or two ahead and stored, covered, in the fridge.

Serve it with
    ✦ A platter of assorted cheese and crusty bread
    ✦ Grilled or roasted pork loin
    ✦ Roasted Salmon with Garlic Confit (page 107)

Change it up
    ✦ Add 3 to 4 cups mixed greens (arugula, baby spinach, chopped romaine, etc.) for a larger, lighter salad.

Warm Jerusalem Artichoke Salad

Also called "sunchoke," this knobby, gingerroot-looking, winter vegetable is not related to the artichoke at all, but is actually the tuber of a type of sunflower. The "Jerusalem" part of the name comes from the Italian word for sunflower, *girasole*. Jerusalem artichokes have a light, sweet, nutty flavor and a potato-like texture. They can be boiled, mashed, baked, sautéed, dropped into stews, puréed into soups, and even eaten raw. The skin doesn't need to be peeled—it's thin *and* nutritious—but be sure to scrub well. Note that aluminum or iron pans will cause oxidation and turn the 'chokes a dark, unappetizing color.

1½ pounds Jerusalem artichokes, scrubbed and sliced ¼ inch thick
¼ medium red onion, thinly sliced
2 tablespoons capers, drained
¼ cup (tightly packed) chopped fresh mint
Lemon Vinaigrette (page 148)

Place Jerusalem artichokes in a pot with just enough water to cover them and bring to a boil. Reduce heat to medium and boil gently until artichokes are easily pierced with a fork, 5 to 7 minutes more. Transfer to a colander to drain and let cool for 5 minutes. In a serving bowl, toss artichokes with onion, capers, mint, and vinaigrette to taste. Serve immediately.

Serves 4 to 6.

Change it up
+ Top with crumbled feta cheese.

Chilled Soba Noodle Salad with Shrimp, Avocado, and Grapefruit in Wasabi-Lime Vinaigrette

Spicy Japanese wasabi paste gives our Wasabi-Lime Vinaigrette (page 151) its unique flavor. Tart lime and grapefruit, rich avocado, and savory shrimp complete the picture of a perfect main course salad.

> 12 ounces soba (Japanese buckwheat) noodles
> Wasabi-Lime Vinaigrette (page 151)
> 1 ruby grapefruit
> 1 medium Hass avocado (the kind with bumpy black skin), peeled, pitted, and diced
> 4–6 radishes, halved lengthwise and thinly sliced
> 1 medium cucumber, peeled, quartered lengthwise, and thinly sliced crosswise
> 2 green onions, white and pale green part only, thinly sliced
> 1 pound cooked, peeled shrimp

Cook soba noodles according to package instructions. Drain in a colander, rinse well with cold water, and drain thoroughly. In a large bowl, toss the noodles with about ¼ cup vinaigrette.

Using a sharp knife, cut the peel, including all the white pith, from the grapefruit and then cut the segments of flesh from the membranes and set on a double layer of paper towels to drain.

Divide the noodles among 4 serving plates. Top with the avocado, radishes, cucumber, green onions, and grapefruit sections, dividing evenly. Pile a quarter of the shrimp on each of the 4 salads. Drizzle vinaigrette over the salads to taste, and serve.

Serves 4.

Make it ahead

The noodles can be cooked a day ahead and kept, covered, in the fridge.

Change it up

- ✦ For a more decadent salad, replace the shrimp with the sliced meat from 2 lobster tails.
- ✦ For a lighter salad, replace the noodles with 6 cups of mâche or other delicate salad greens.

Chapter Six

SOUPS

Caramelized Onion Soup with Parmesan Lace

Caramelized onions add something special to any dish they accompany. Why not make them the featured attraction? This comforting, robust soup lets them take center stage, in all their rich, sweet, savory glory.

¼ cup (½ stick) unsalted butter
2 pounds yellow onions, thinly sliced
2 garlic cloves, minced
½ teaspoon kosher salt
1 teaspoon freshly ground pepper
1 teaspoon dried thyme
1 tablespoon flour
½ cup red wine
6 cups beef broth
Parmesan Lace (page 161), for garnish

Melt butter in a stockpot over medium heat until it is melted and beginning to bubble. Add onions and garlic and cook, stirring often, until onions are soft and golden brown (30 to 40 minutes). Add salt, pepper, thyme, and flour and cook, stirring, 1 minute. Add wine and broth, increase heat to medium-high, and bring to a boil. Reduce heat to medium and simmer 10 to 12 minutes, until soup is reduced a little and flavors start to meld. Taste, and add additional salt and pepper if needed.

Ladle soup into serving bowls, garnish each with a few pieces of parmesan lace, and serve immediately.

Serves 4 to 6.

Asian Yellow Gazpacho with Spicy Cilantro Pesto

When it's so hot that you don't even want to turn on the stove, this refreshing soup is just the thing. With its striking color combination and bright, refreshing flavors, it's the perfect dish for a summer day.

1 pound yellow tomatoes, stem ends removed, quartered
2 cups chopped seedless yellow watermelon
1 yellow bell pepper, stemmed, seeded, and chopped
1 medium cucumber, peeled, seeded, and chopped
1 medium shallot, peeled and quartered
3 cloves garlic, peeled, divided
2 tablespoons unseasoned rice wine vinegar
1 teaspoon kosher salt
¼–½ teaspoon freshly ground black pepper
3 cups (packed) fresh cilantro (leaves and stems)
2 serrano chiles, stemmed and seeded
1 tablespoon sugar
¼ cup olive oil
2 tablespoons lime juice (from about 1½ limes)
1 tablespoon fish sauce or soy sauce

In a blender or food processor, combine the tomatoes, watermelon, bell pepper, cucumber, shallot, 2 cloves of garlic, rice vinegar, salt, and pepper and process to a chunky purée. Pour into a pitcher or bowl and refrigerate, covered, until well chilled (at least 2 hours or overnight).

Give the blender or food processor a quick rinse and then add the cilantro, remaining clove of garlic, and chiles and process until minced. Add the sugar, olive oil, lime juice, and fish sauce or soy sauce and process to a fairly smooth purée.

Ladle the chilled soup into bowls, garnish with a dollop of pesto, and serve.

Serves 4 to 6.

Make it ahead

The soup and the pesto can be stored in separate covered containers in the fridge for a couple of days.

Serve it with

+ A spicy shrimp salad and tortilla chips
+ Scallop Ceviche with Papaya and Chiles (page 51)
+ Chilled Soba Noodle Salad with Shrimp, Avocado, and Grapefruit in Wasabi-Lime Vinaigrette (page 151)

White Gazpacho

This traditional Spanish soup is less famous than its tomato-based kin, but just as wonderful. Its unassuming milky whiteness and silky-smooth texture conceal serious flavor. Serve chilled, with a garnish of green grapes and almonds and additional bread to dip. And don't tell any Spaniards we said this, but it's also good warmed up.

4 cups bread cubes from rustic white bread, crusts removed
3½ cups cold water
1½ cups blanched almonds, divided
1½ cups seedless green grapes, divided
1–3 small cloves garlic, peeled
¼ cup olive oil
2 tablespoons sherry vinegar
½ teaspoon kosher salt

Combine the bread and water in a bowl and let soak for 5 to 10 minutes. In a blender or food processor, purée bread, water, 1 cup almonds, ½ cup grapes, 1 clove of garlic, olive oil, vinegar, and salt. Taste and add the additional 1 or 2 cloves of garlic if desired.

Continue blending until mixture is almost perfectly smooth. Strain through a fine-meshed sieve or strainer, taste, and add additional salt if needed.

Serve chilled, garnished with the remaining almonds and grapes.

Serves 4.

Make it ahead

Make this soup a day ahead and it will only get better as the flavors meld.

Garlic Soup with Asparagus and Poached Eggs

The famous food author and editor Ruth Reichl said it best: "If everyone ate more garlic, the world would be a happy place." This rich, garlicky broth, boasting a minimum of seven cloves of garlic per serving and studded with bright green asparagus and shimmering poached eggs, will make you and yours very happy, indeed.

2 tablespoons olive oil
2 small heads garlic (about 20–22 cloves), cloves separated, peeled,
    and smashed with the side of a broad knife
6 cups low-sodium chicken or vegetable broth
½–1 teaspoon kosher salt (depending on the saltiness of your broth)
1 pound asparagus, woody ends snapped off, cut into 1-inch lengths
2 large eggs
freshly grated Parmesan cheese for serving
freshly ground black pepper for serving

Heat oil in a stockpot over low heat. Add garlic and cook, stirring occasionally, about 10 to 12 minutes, until just barely beginning to turn golden brown. Add broth and ½ teaspoon salt and bring to a boil. Reduce heat to low and simmer, stirring occasionally, about 60 minutes, until broth is fully infused with garlic flavor.

Remove garlic cloves with a slotted spoon. Taste, and add additional salt if needed. If more garlic flavor is desired, mash 6 to 8 (or more) of the cooked garlic cloves with the back of a fork and stir into the broth. Raise heat to medium-high and bring to a boil. Reduce heat to medium, add asparagus, and cook about 3 minutes.

Crack the eggs into the soup. Simmer the eggs and asparagus in the broth for 4 minutes more, until asparagus is tender and egg is poached but the yolk is still runny. Ladle the soup into two bowls, placing one egg in each. Top with freshly grated Parmesan and freshly ground pepper, and serve immediately.

Serves 2.

Make it ahead

The soup can be made a couple of days in advance up to the point of adding the asparagus. Store, covered, in the fridge. When ready to serve, bring the broth to a boil over medium-high heat, add asparagus, and follow the rest of the instructions.

Serve it with

✦ Toasted rustic bread, such as walnut levain or whole wheat sourdough

Change it up

✦ Instead of the eggs, add one 15-ounce can butter beans or lima beans, drained and rinsed.

Spring Leek, Pea, and Lettuce Soup

Who would have thought that lettuce would be so delicious cooked and puréed into a soup? Light and refreshing, it will delight your guests and the surprise factor will give them something to talk about, too.

2 tablespoons olive oil
2 cloves garlic, minced
2 medium leeks (white and pale green part only), trimmed, halved lengthwise, and thinly sliced
5 cups (loosely packed) romaine lettuce, chopped
1 cup fresh or frozen peas
3½ cups chicken or vegetable broth, plus additional to thin soup if desired
½ teaspoon salt
¼–½ teaspoon freshly ground black pepper
½ teaspoon sugar
½ cup half-and-half

In a large, heavy pot, heat oil over medium-high heat. Add garlic and leeks and cook until leeks are soft, 4 to 5 minutes. Stir in lettuce and peas and cook, stirring, until lettuce wilts, about 3 to 4 minutes more. Add broth, salt, pepper, and sugar and bring to a boil. Lower heat and simmer about 10 minutes. Using an immersion blender (or in batches in a countertop blender or food processor), purée the soup until smooth. If using a blender, return soup to pot. Just before serving, reheat and whisk in half-and-half. Taste, and add additional salt and pepper if needed.

Serves 4 to 6.

Make it ahead

The soup can be made a couple of days in advance up to and including the puréeing. Store, covered, in the fridge until ready to serve. Before serving, reheat over medium heat until warmed, and add half-and-half.

Cilantro-Spinach Soup with Crunchy Croutons

This light, refreshing soup is a great way to get your cilantro fix without having to fuss with de-stemming or chopping those tiny leaves. We recommend making your own Homemade Croutons (page 163), but a good-quality store-bought variety will work fine, too.

2 tablespoons olive oil
1 large onion, diced
2 cloves garlic, minced
½ teaspoon kosher salt
¼–½ teaspoon freshly ground black pepper
2 medium potatoes (about 1¼ pounds), chopped
6 cups chicken or vegetable broth
1 pound fresh spinach leaves
1 cup (tightly packed) fresh cilantro (leaves and stems)
1 cup buttermilk
crème fraîche, sour cream, or plain yogurt, for garnish
Homemade Croutons (page 163), for garnish
3 green onions, white and pale green parts only, thinly sliced, for garnish

In a stockpot, heat oil over medium-high heat. When oil is hot but not smoking, add onions, garlic, salt, and pepper. Cook, stirring frequently, until onions are soft and translucent (5 to 7 minutes). Add potatoes and stock and bring to a boil. Reduce heat to low, cover, and simmer until potatoes are soft (15 to 20 minutes). Add spinach. If you can't fit it all in the pot at once, add it in handfuls, letting one bunch cook for a few seconds before adding the next. When spinach is wilted, after 3 to 4 minutes, add cilantro.

Using an immersion blender (or in batches in a countertop blender or food processor), purée the soup until smooth. Stir in buttermilk and reheat if needed. Taste, and add additional salt and pepper if needed.

Ladle soup into serving bowls, garnish with a dollop of crème fraîche, sour cream, or yogurt, and sprinkle with a few croutons and sliced green onions.

Serves 6 to 8.

Make it ahead

The soup can be made one day ahead up to and including the puréeing and stored, covered, in the fridge. Before serving, heat over medium heat and then add buttermilk and taste for seasoning.

Roasted Cauliflower Soup with Truffle Oil
. . . .

There's no better way to kick off a winter meal than with a cream-of-something soup. In this case the something is roasted cauliflower, whose rich, nutty flavor is a perfect starter to a steak or pork dinner. A drizzle of truffle oil provides a whole lot of flavor—and sophistication.

> 1 head cauliflower (about 1½ pounds florets), cut into small chunks
> 1 medium yellow or white onion, cut into wedges
> olive oil or olive oil spray
> 4 cups chicken or vegetable broth
> ½ teaspoon kosher salt
> ½ teaspoon freshly ground black pepper
> ¼ cup heavy cream
> 1 tablespoon truffle oil, plus more for garnish

Preheat oven to 450°F.

Spread cauliflower and onion on a baking sheet and brush, drizzle, or spray with olive oil to coat thoroughly. Roast in preheated oven for 35 to 45 minutes, stirring once about halfway through, until cauliflower is tender and beginning to brown.

In a stockpot, combine the cauliflower, onion, and broth. Using an immersion blender (or in batches in a countertop blender or food processor), purée the soup until smooth. Heat soup over medium-high heat to just below boiling. Stir in the salt, pepper, cream, and truffle oil. Taste, and add additional salt and pepper if needed. Ladle into soup bowls and garnish each with an extra swirl of truffle oil. Serve immediately.

Serves 4.

Make it ahead
> The soup can be made a couple of days in advance without adding the truffle oil. Store, covered, in the fridge until ready to serve. Before serving, reheat over medium heat until warmed, and continue following instructions.

Roasted Tomato-Curry Soup

Roasting the tomatoes, along with garlic and curry powder, gives an unexpected twist to a standard favorite.

 3 pounds Roma tomatoes, halved, stem ends removed
 1 large onion, coarsely chopped
 8 medium cloves garlic, peeled
 2 tablespoons olive oil
 1 teaspoon kosher salt
 1 teaspoon freshly ground black pepper
 3 tablespoons curry powder
 4 cups chicken or vegetable broth
 ½ cup half-and-half or heavy cream
 3 tablespoons lemon juice (from about 1 lemon)
 Whole cilantro leaves, for garnish

Preheat oven to 450°F.

In a large baking dish, toss tomatoes, onions, and garlic with olive oil, salt, pepper, and curry powder. Roast in preheated oven for 40 to 50 minutes, stirring occasionally, until vegetables are very soft.

Working in batches, place vegetables and their juices in a blender or food processor with the broth and blend until smooth. (If you prefer to use an immersion blender, simply place the roasted vegetables, their juices, and the broth in a large pot and blend it there.) Pour into a large pot, bring to a simmer over medium heat, and stir in half-and-half or heavy cream and lemon juice. Taste, and add additional salt and pepper if needed. Serve hot, garnished with cilantro leaves.

Serves 4 to 6.

Make it ahead

 The soup can be made a couple of days ahead up to and including the blending and stored, covered, in the fridge. Before serving, heat over medium heat and continue following instructions.

Change it up

 ✦ Substitute fresh thyme leaves for the curry powder and garnish with minced parsley.

Parsnip and Apple Soup

Earthy parsnips and sweet apples combine to make a perfectly sublime soup. The vegetables and apples can all be coarsely chopped since they'll be puréed in the end anyway, making preparation a breeze!

    2 tablespoons unsalted butter
    2 tablespoons olive oil
    1½ pounds parsnips, peeled and chopped
    2 large apples (any type), peeled, cored, and chopped
    1 medium potato, peeled and chopped
    3 medium shallots, chopped
    1 teaspoon kosher salt
    ¼–½ teaspoon freshly ground black pepper
    5 cups chicken or vegetable broth
    ½ cup heavy cream
    Homemade Croutons (regular, or the blue cheese variation) (page 163)
        or Parmesan Lace (page 161) for garnish

In a stockpot, heat the butter and olive oil over medium-high heat until butter is melted and bubbling. Add the parsnips, apples, potatoes, shallots, salt, and pepper, and cook, stirring occasionally, about 8 to 10 minutes. Add broth and bring to a boil over high heat. Reduce heat to medium-low, cover, and simmer until the parsnips and potatoes are soft, about 20 minutes. Using an immersion blender (or in batches in a countertop blender or food processor), purée the soup until smooth. Stir in cream, taste, and add additional salt and pepper if needed. Serve hot, garnished with croutons or lace.

Serves 4 to 6.

Make it ahead

The soup can be made a couple of days ahead up to and including the puréeing. Store, covered, in the fridge until ready to serve. Before serving, reheat over medium heat and stir in the cream.

Cod and Chickpea Soup with Garlic Aioli

Partnered with hot, crusty bread, this light yet satisfying soup is a complete meal in a bowl.

2 tablespoons olive oil
1 large onion, diced
6 cloves garlic, minced, divided
⅛–½ teaspoon cayenne pepper, or to taste
1 teaspoon kosher salt, divided
¼–½ teaspoon freshly ground black pepper
2 bay leaves
1 28-ounce can diced tomatoes with their juice
1 cup red wine
4 cups chicken broth or fish stock
¼ cup tomato paste
1 15-ounce can chickpeas (garbanzo beans), rinsed and drained
1 pound cod fillets, cut into 1-inch pieces
¾ cup mayonnaise
2 tablespoons minced fresh oregano
minced flat leaf parsley, for garnish

In a stockpot, heat oil over medium-high heat. When oil is hot but not smoking, add onion and half of the garlic and stir until onions are soft and translucent, 5 to 7 minutes. Add cayenne, ½ teaspoon salt, pepper, bay leaves, tomatoes, wine, broth or stock, tomato paste, and chickpeas, and bring to a boil. Reduce heat to medium-low and simmer, covered, for 30 minutes.

Add fish and continue to simmer until fish is cooked through and flakes easily with a fork, 3 to 5 minutes.

While fish is cooking, make the garlic aioli. Combine the mayonnaise with the remaining garlic and ½ teaspoon salt in a small bowl, stirring to mix well. Set aside.

Stir oregano into soup, taste, and add additional salt and pepper if needed. Ladle soup into bowls and top each with a dollop of garlic aioli and a sprinkling of parsley. Serve immediately.

Serves 4 to 6.

Make it ahead

The soup can be made a couple of days ahead up to and including the 30 minutes of simmering (but without adding the chickpeas) and stored, covered, in the fridge. When you're ready to serve it, heat it back up to a simmer on the stove, add chickpeas and fish, and follow the rest of the instructions.

Serve it with

✦ Lots of crusty bread for dunking and a crisp green salad

Change it up

✦ Substitute another meaty white fish, such as halibut or snapper, or a mixture of seafood, such as clams, shrimp, squid, and crab.

Chapter Seven

SANDWICHES

Radish and Watercress Tea Sandwiches

Fancy, crustless little white bread sandwiches are perfect for tea parties, luncheons, or just a special snack. Lemon juice is one of our favorite companions for cream cheese—you'll soon discover why.

> 8 slices soft white bread, crusts removed
> ½ cup cream cheese
> ¼ cup thinly sliced green onions
> ½ cup (tightly packed) watercress leaves
> 5–7 medium radishes, thinly sliced
> 3 tablespoons lemon juice (from about 1 lemon)
> kosher salt to taste
> freshly ground black pepper to taste

Spread cream cheese on 4 bread slices. Top with green onions, watercress, and radish slices, dividing evenly. Drizzle lemon juice on each sandwich and sprinkle with salt and pepper to taste. Cover with remaining bread slices and cut each sandwich along both diagonals to create 4 small triangles.

Makes 16 mini sandwiches.

Smoked Herring Smörgås

The Scandinavian open-faced sandwich (smørrebrød, smørbrød, and smörgås to the Danes, Norwegians, and Swedes) is a diverse and adaptable tradition. Simply butter a piece of hearty dark bread and pile it neatly with your favorite meat, fish, vegetables, cheese, eggs, herbs, and whatever else you fancy. Cocktail-sized, sliced pumpernickel loaves are available at many supermarkets and delis—but if you can't find them, just get a large square loaf and cut four slices into quarters. You can also use crispy rye crackerbreads made by companies like Kavli or Wasa.

16 cocktail-sized (about 2½ inches square) slices of pumpernickel bread
3–4 tablespoons unsalted butter, softened
16 large cucumber slices
4 hard-boiled eggs, sliced
1 7-ounce can smoked herring fillets, cut into 1-inch squares about ¼ inch thick
kosher salt to taste
freshly ground black pepper to taste
1–2 large sprigs of fresh dill

Generously butter each piece of bread. Stack a slice of cucumber, a slice of egg (from the middle of the egg, so it includes some yolk), and a piece of fish on the buttered bread. Sprinkle with salt and pepper, to taste, and top with a sprig or two of dill.

Makes 16 mini sandwiches.

Roasted Vegetable Sandwich with St. André Triple Cream Cheese

Roast a load of vegetables for dinner (see Roasted Vegetables with Balsamic Syrup, page 138), and make these sandwiches for lunch the next day. St. André triple cream is a soft-ripened cheese, like Brie, but with a dense, buttery consistency and a decadent, creamy taste. It's carried in many supermarkets, but if you can't find it you can substitute Brie.

> 3 pounds mixed vegetables (such as zucchini, summer squash, mushrooms, eggplant,
>   asparagus, or bell peppers), roasted (see page 138 for roasting instructions)
> 4–6 ounces St. André triple cream cheese, well chilled
> 8 slices rustic French bread, lightly toasted

Chop any large pieces, and mix roasted vegetables in a large bowl. (You don't need to chop asparagus or radicchio—use your judgment.) Layer vegetables and slices of cheese onto each sandwich, dividing evenly.

Makes 4 sandwiches.

Change it up

+ Make open-faced crostini using slices of batard or another medium-width bread. Garnish with a couple of leaves of baby spinach or arugula.
+ Drizzle a little Balsamic Syrup (page 147) on sandwiches.

Portobello Mushroom Sandwiches

Portobello mushroom caps—with their burger-like shape, strong flavor, and sturdy texture—simply beg to be sandwiched. To clean portobello mushroom caps, gently wipe them with a clean, damp paper towel. To remove the stem, just grab hold of it and bend until it breaks off naturally. For best bread-to-filling ratio, choose a bun or roll that has a diameter at least as wide as the mushroom cap, but is not too dense.

4 sandwich-sized Portobello mushroom, cleaned and stemmed
olive oil or olive oil spray
¾ teaspoon kosher salt, divided
¼–½ teaspoon freshly ground black pepper
1 15-ounce can white beans, such as butter beans, cannellini, or navy beans, drained and rinsed
1 tablespoon olive oil
1 medium clove garlic, minced
½ cup store-bought julienned, roasted red bell peppers
2 handfuls of arugula leaves
8–12 large basil leaves
4 good-quality hamburger buns or sandwich rolls, toasted

Preheat oven to 400°F.

Brush or spray mushroom caps with olive oil and place them on a baking sheet, top sides up. Sprinkle with pepper and ¼ teaspoon salt. Bake about 20 minutes, until mushrooms are browned and a little shrunken.

In a small bowl with a fork, mash beans with olive oil, garlic, and remaining ½ teaspoon salt to make a chunky purée. Spread the bean mixture onto the bottom halves of the buns, dividing equally, and layer the red peppers, arugula, basil, and mushrooms on top, dividing them equally among the 4 sandwiches. Top each sandwich with the top half of the bun, and serve immediately, while the mushrooms are still warm.

Makes 4 sandwiches.

Serve it with
✦ Heirloom Tomato Salad with Feta, Chives, and Pine Nuts (page 62)
✦ Sweet potato fries

Bombay-Style Vegetable Sandwiches

Our friend and home chef Aneela Brister gave us the idea for this version of a sandwich sold by street vendors in her hometown, Bombay (now Mumbai). You can use any white bread, but for tastiest results we recommend buttermilk bread, which is slightly sweet.

12 ounces small new potatoes (red- or white-skinned)
8 slices soft white bread, such as buttermilk, crusts removed
½ cup Spiced Yogurt-Cilantro Sauce (page 157)
1 small cucumber, peeled and thinly sliced
1 large tomato, thinly sliced
kosher salt to taste
freshly ground black pepper, to taste
2 tablespoons unsalted butter, softened

Place potatoes on a microwave-safe plate and microwave on high until cooked through, anywhere from 5 to 10 minutes, depending on the size of your potatoes and the power of your microwave. (Cook for intervals of 1 or 2 minutes, checking to see if they're cooked through by poking with a fork, which should penetrate easily.) When potatoes are cooked, slice them into thin discs.

Spread a quarter of the yogurt-cilantro sauce (about 2 tablespoons per sandwich) on each of 4 bread slices. Layer the sliced potatoes, tomatoes, and cucumber on top, dividing equally and salting each layer lightly. Grind pepper over the top layer. Spread butter on the remaining 4 slices of bread, dividing equally, and place atop the sandwiches, butter side down, pressing firmly. Cut each sandwich along both diagonals to create 4 small triangles.

Makes 16 mini sandwiches.

Change it up
+ Add sliced red onions or sliced roasted beets.
+ Try grilling the sandwiches, panini style.

Herbed Tuna Salad Sandwiches with Apples and Almonds

This version of a familiar favorite surprises and delights with the unexpected addition of tart green apple, crunchy almonds, and fresh herbs.

    2 6-ounce cans of solid white tuna, drained
    1 medium Granny Smith or other crisp, tart apple, cored and diced
    2 tablespoons minced red onion
    2 teaspoons minced fresh thyme or oregano
    ¼ cup toasted slivered almonds
    3 tablespoons lemon juice (from about 1 lemon)
    ½ teaspoon kosher salt
    ¼–½ teaspoon freshly ground black pepper
    ¼ cup mayonnaise
    1 teaspoon Dijon mustard
    8 slices rustic whole wheat sourdough or levain bread
    8 small or 4 large radicchio leaves

In a medium bowl, mix the tuna, apple, onion, herbs, almonds, lemon juice, salt, and pepper. Toss until thoroughly combined, and stir in the mayonnaise and mustard.

Lightly toast the bread, and lay 4 slices on your work surface. Divide the tuna mixture evenly among the bread slices and top each with 1 or 2 radicchio leaves. Top with the remaining bread slices. Cut each sandwich in half, and serve immediately.

Makes 4 sandwiches.

Make it ahead

The tuna mixture can be made up to a day ahead and stored, covered, in the fridge. Toast bread and assemble sandwiches just before serving.

Serve it with
- ✦ Spicy Pickled Carrots (page 35)
- ✦ A salad of baby greens and tomato tossed with Balsamic Vinaigrette (page 149)
- ✦ A handful of good-quality potato chips

Change it up
- ✦ Substitute halved seedless red grapes for the apples.
- ✦ Add 1 tablespoon of curry powder in place of the fresh herbs and add ¼ to ½ teaspoon cayenne, if desired.

Olive and Sun-Dried Tomato Tapenade Sandwich

Our Olive and Sun-Dried Tomato Tapenade (page 46) can be prepared several days in advance, making this sandwich easy to throw together right before serving. It's perfect for a fancy bag lunch or picnic.

1 10-ounce baguette, sliced in half horizontally and lightly toasted
4 ounces chèvre
¾ cup Olive and Sun-Dried Tomato Tapenade (page 46)
2 Roma tomatoes, sliced
4–6 small romaine lettuce leaves

Spread chèvre on bottom half of baguette. Layer tapenade, tomato slices, and lettuce on top of the cheese. Close sandwich with the top half of the baguette and slice into 4 or 8 individual sandwiches.

Makes 4 large sandwiches or 8 small sandwiches.

Prosciutto and Taleggio Sandwich with Lemon-Raisin Salsa

Sweet, salty, spicy, and tangy, this sandwich has it all. Taleggio is an Italian semisoft aged cow's milk cheese. It's rich and creamy, with both fruity and nutty notes. If you can't find Taleggio, the milder Fontina is a decent substitute.

> **2 ciabatta rolls**
> **6 ounces Taleggio cheese, sliced**
> **Lemon-Raisin Salsa (page 154)**
> **4 ounces (8 slices) prosciutto**
> **2 cups (loosely packed) arugula leaves**

Split rolls and toast them until golden brown. While rolls are still hot, place the cheese on the bottom halves, dividing evenly. Spoon the salsa on top of the cheese, again dividing evenly, and drape 4 slices of prosciutto on each sandwich. (It should be rumpled like the sheets of an unmade bed.) Top with arugula. Place the top halves of the rolls on the sandwiches, cut each sandwich in half, and serve.

Makes 2 sandwiches.

Prosciutto, Asparagus, and Fried Egg Sandwich

Adapted from a tattered old Italian cookbook, "THE Sandwich" was given its nickname by the envious co-workers who used to watch it baking in the toaster oven at one of our former workplaces. If you bring THE Sandwich to work, you too can become a lunchroom legend!

1 pound slender asparagus, woody ends snapped off
olive oil or olive oil spray
¾ teaspoon kosher salt, divided
1 tablespoon butter
4 large eggs
4 slices hearty, rustic bread, toasted lightly
8–12 slices prosciutto
2 ounces (about ⅔ cup) grated Gruyère cheese
freshly ground black pepper, to taste

Preheat oven to 400°F.

Place asparagus spears in a single layer on a baking sheet. Drizzle or spray with olive oil, turning spears to coat thoroughly. Sprinkle with ½ teaspoon salt. Roast in preheated oven for 10 to 15 minutes, depending on thickness of the spears, until almost tender.

While asparagus is roasting, heat butter in a heavy skillet over medium-high heat until melted and starting to bubble. Fry eggs to desired doneness. Top each slice of toast with prosciutto, one fried egg, a few spears of asparagus, and cheese, dividing evenly. (You may need to trim the asparagus to fit the toast.) Season with pepper and remaining salt. Place sandwiches on the baking sheet and bake another 5 minutes, until cheese is just slightly melted.

Makes 4 sandwiches.

Make it ahead

Assemble sandwiches ahead and bake them when ready to eat.

BLT with Wasabi Mayonnaise

The classic BLT is elevated a notch or two with spicy wasabi mayonnaise and peppery arugula. Wasabi paste, the Japanese condiment served with sushi, can be found in the Asian foods aisle of many supermarkets or in Asian specialty markets, either in paste or powder form (just mix with equal parts water). If you have the option, choose arugula that tends toward the bitter, peppery end of the arugula flavor spectrum.

⅔ cup mayonnaise
1–2 tablespoons wasabi paste
a couple of handfuls of arugula leaves
12 strips crispy cooked bacon
2 medium tomatoes, sliced
1-pound loaf focaccia bread, cut into four sandwich-sized rectangles,
    each sliced in half horizontally and lightly toasted

In a small bowl, mix mayonnaise with 1 tablespoon wasabi. Taste mixture and add more wasabi, if desired. Spread mayonnaise mixture on the bottom halves of the focaccia squares. Layer on the arugula, bacon, tomatoes, and focaccia tops.

Makes 4 sandwiches.

Change it up

✦ Add sliced avocado, a familiar partner to wasabi, for an extra rich and flavorful touch.
✦ If you can't find wasabi, spruce up your mayonnaise with some lemon juice, minced garlic, and a pinch of cayenne pepper.

Chapter Eight

SMALL PLATES AND MAIN DISHES

Baked Tilapia with Lemon-Raisin Salsa

Tilapia's mild flavor makes this fish a perfect host for flavorful foils like our sweet-tart Lemon-Raisin Salsa (page 154). And if you're concerned about the environmental implications of consuming fish, rest assured that farmed tilapia is one of the most sustainable, environmentally friendly fish around (and it's low in mercury, too).

2 6-ounce tilapia fillets
½ teaspoon kosher salt
¼–½ teaspoon freshly ground black pepper
Lemon-Raisin Salsa (page 154)

Preheat oven to 375°F. Lightly oil a baking dish.

Place tilapia fillets in prepared baking dish. Sprinkle with salt and pepper. Bake in preheated oven for 12 to 15 minutes, until fish flakes easily with a fork. Top each serving with a helping of Lemon-Raisin Salsa.

Serves 2.

Serve it with
✦ Wild rice or couscous

Meyer Lemon and Asparagus Tart

Meyer lemon slices (page 7), layered under tender asparagus spears and melted Gruyère, add a surprising element to this simple and beautiful tart. Note that it's important to blanch the lemons and slice them paper thin, or you may wind up with a bitter-tasting tart. Be sure to read the section on working with frozen puff pastry (page 14).

> 1 large Meyer lemon
> 1 pound slender asparagus, woody ends snapped off
> 1 sheet frozen puff pastry, defrosted
> 3 ounces grated Gruyère cheese (about 1 cup), divided
> kosher salt to taste
> freshly ground black pepper to taste

Preheat oven to 400°F. Lightly oil a baking sheet.

Drop lemon into boiling water for 1 minute to blanch. Run under cold water and set in fridge to cool. After a few minutes of cooling, use a very sharp knife to slice lemon into paper-thin slices. Remove and discard seeds. Trim the ends of the asparagus spears, cutting them to equal lengths so they'll look nice lying side by side in the tart.

Unfold the pastry sheet on a lightly floured surface. You'll want the pastry sheet to be a square with sides about 2 inches longer than your asparagus spears, so if it's not quite big enough, roll it out a little with a lightly floured rolling pin. Place pastry on prepared baking sheet. Using a fork, pierce dough at ½-inch intervals, leaving a 1-inch unpierced border around the outside.

Sprinkle half of the grated cheese inside the border. Place lemon slices in a single layer on top of the cheese. Arrange asparagus spears in a neat row on top of the lemons, alternating the orientation of the tips and ends so that if the tart is cut into quarters no one gets stuck with an ends-only piece. Top with the remaining cheese and sprinkle with salt and pepper.

Bake in preheated oven for 20 to 25 minutes, or until asparagus is tender and pastry is golden brown and nicely puffed up around the edges. Serve warm.

Serves 4.

Make it ahead

Tarts are best served right out of the oven, but if you want to enjoy them as leftovers they can be reheated at 400°F until heated through (about 5 minutes).

Serve it with
- ✦ Salad of Bitter Greens with Asiago (page 60)
- ✦ Any simple salad of mixed greens tossed with a light vinaigrette

Change it up
- ✦ Substitute chèvre, Emmentaler, or another flavorful cheese for the Gruyère.

Lazy Cheese Soufflés

Your guests will swoon when you serve them these smooth, creamy custards in individual ramekins. They're a perfect start for a fancy dinner or, served with a crisp green salad and warm crusty bread, as the main event for a special lunch. For a dramatic visual presentation, serve immediately, while the tops are still puffed up. But don't worry if they collapse before they get to the table— they'll still look beautiful and taste great.

3 large eggs
1 cup whole milk
½ cup heavy cream
¼ teaspoon kosher salt
¼ teaspoon ground nutmeg
¼–½ teaspoon cayenne pepper
¾ cup grated Gruyère cheese (about 2½ ounces)
½ cup grated Parmesan cheese (about 1½ ounces)

Preheat oven to 350°F. Boil water in a kettle. Oil six 4-ounce (½-cup) ramekins. Place ramekins in a baking dish.

In a large bowl, whisk the eggs, milk, cream, salt, nutmeg, and cayenne until well blended. Stir in the cheeses. Ladle mixture into prepared ramekins. Pour boiling water into the baking dish until it comes halfway up the sides of the ramekins. Bake until the tops are puffed up and golden, 50 to 60 minutes.

Serves 6.

Serve it with
- ✦ Raw Asparagus and Mâche Salad with Citrus Vinaigrette (page 58)
- ✦ Cilantro-Spinach Soup with Crunchy Croutons (page 74)

Apple, Blue Cheese, and Walnut Tarts

Your guests will think you're a real pro when you pull these sweet, savory, golden-crusted little tarts out of the oven. We recommend using a milder blue cheese like Cambozola, but feel free to experiment with stronger varieties if you like. Crisp red-skinned apples, like Pink Ladies or Fujis, are especially pretty here. Be sure to read the section on working with frozen puff pastry (page 14).

1 sheet frozen puff pastry, defrosted
1 medium apple, quartered, cored, and sliced into ⅛-inch-thick slices
4 ounces Cambozola or other blue cheese, thinly sliced or crumbled
¼ cup chopped walnuts
1 tablespoon honey
freshly ground black pepper

Preheat oven to 400°F. Lightly oil a baking sheet.

Unfold the pastry sheet on a lightly floured surface. Cut sheet into four squares and place on prepared baking sheet. Using a fork, pierce dough at ½-inch intervals, leaving a 1-inch unpierced border around the outside.

Lay 4 apple slices, slightly overlapping, in the center of each square (you may have apple left over), followed by the cheese, walnuts, and a drizzle of honey, dividing evenly. Grind pepper over each tart. Bake in preheated oven for 15 to 20 minutes, until pastry is golden brown and nicely puffed up around the edges. Serve warm.

Makes 4 tarts.

Make it ahead

Tarts are best served right out of the oven, but if you want to enjoy them as leftovers they can be reheated at 400°F until heated through (about 5 minutes).

Serve it with

✦ A mixed green salad with Lemon Vinaigrette (page 148) or Sherry-Shallot Vinaigrette (page 150)

Change it up

✦ Substitute figs, apricots, or pears for the apple.
✦ Substitute grated Gruyère, sharp white Cheddar, or Manchego for the Cambozola.
✦ Turn this dish into dessert by substituting ricotta for the blue cheese and omitting the pepper.

Savory Pumpkin and Sage Flan

Whip out your trusty ramekins and whip up this savory flan for your next dinner party. A perfect accompaniment to a hearty winter dinner.

2 large eggs, lightly beaten
½ cup whole milk
¼ cup (about 1 ounce) grated Parmesan cheese
1 15-ounce can puréed pumpkin
2 tablespoons maple syrup
¼–½ teaspoon cayenne pepper
1 teaspoon kosher salt
¼–½ teaspoon freshly ground black pepper
1 tablespoon (tightly packed) minced fresh sage leaves

Preheat oven to 400°F. Boil about 2 cups of water. Lightly oil four 8-ounce (1-cup) ramekins.

In a large bowl, mix eggs, milk, cheese, puréed pumpkin, syrup, cayenne, salt, pepper, and sage leaves until well combined.

Place ramekins in a 2-inch-deep baking pan. Fill each ramekin almost to the top (leave about ⅛ inch) with the pumpkin mixture. Pour boiling water into the pan until it comes about halfway up the sides of the ramekins. Bake about 45 minutes, until a wooden toothpick inserted in the center of one of the ramekins comes out almost clean.

To serve, run a knife around the edge of each flan, invert a plate over the ramekin, and then turn it over. Flans should come out easily. Or just serve the flans right in the ramekins after they've cooled down a bit.

Serves 4.

Make it ahead

Flan can be made a couple of days ahead and stored in the fridge in the ramekins, covered with plastic wrap. To serve, bring to room temperature and reheat at 375°F until heated through, about 10 minutes.

Serve it with

◆ Salad of Bitter Greens with Asiago (page 60)
◆ Broccoli Rabe Sautéed with Garlic and Hot Pepper (page 135)

Change it up

◆ Garnish with Crispy Fried Sage Leaves (page 160).

Creamy Baked Scallops with Capers

Bring a little bit of New England to wherever you are with these tasty seafood appetizers. The individual servings are perfect as a starter or part of a small-plate lunch or dinner. For this recipe, frozen scallops are a fine substitute for fresh.

1 pound small bay scallops (or diced large sea scallops), rinsed and patted dry
3 tablespoons sour cream
2 tablespoons capers, drained
grated zest of 1 lemon
2 tablespoons minced flat leaf parsley
½ teaspoon kosher salt
¼–½ teaspoon freshly ground black pepper
¼ cup breadcrumbs
¼ cup (lightly packed) freshly grated Parmesan cheese (about ½ ounce)

Preheat oven to 400°F. Lightly oil six 4-ounce (½-cup) ramekins.

In a medium bowl, combine scallops, sour cream, capers, zest, parsley, salt, and pepper. In a small bowl, combine breadcrumbs and cheese. Place the ramekins on a baking sheet for easy transfer in and out of the oven. Scoop scallop mixture into ramekins, dividing evenly, and sprinkle breadcrumb mixture over the tops.

Bake in preheated oven until scallops are just cooked through and breadcrumbs are lightly browned, 20 to 25 minutes.

Serves 6.

Make it ahead

The scallop mixture can be made and scooped into ramekins several hours ahead and stored, covered, in the fridge. Top with breadcrumb and cheese mixture just before baking. Note that cold ramekins will increase cooking time, so factor in several extra minutes.

Serve it with

✦ Lightly toasted sourdough bread and Slow-Roasted Tomatoes (page 43) or sliced fresh tomatoes

Change it up

✦ Add ¼ to ½ teaspoon cayenne with the other seasonings.
✦ Replace the parsley with chopped fresh dill, basil, or cilantro.
✦ Use four 8-ounce (1-cup) ramekins to make larger portions, and serve with a mixed salad as a light entrée.

Smoked Trout Brandade

France, Italy, Spain, and Portugal all make regional variations of this dish, traditionally a purée of salt cod, olive oil, milk, and potatoes served as a spread for crusty bread or toast. Here we simplify the technique and substitute smoked trout for a rich, unique flavor.

1½ pounds russet potatoes, peeled and cut into chunks
1 pound smoked trout, skin and any bones removed
¾ cup olive oil
½ cup whole milk, half-and-half, or heavy cream
2 cloves garlic, minced
kosher salt to taste

Bring to a boil a pot of water large enough to hold the potatoes. Add the potatoes and boil until tender, about 15 to 20 minutes. Place trout in a large bowl and, using a fork or your fingers, flake into small pieces. Drain potatoes and add to the fish, mashing well with a fork or potato masher. Slowly work in oil and milk, mashing mixture to a fine, smooth texture. Stir in garlic. Taste, and add salt if needed. Serve warm.

Serves 8 to 10.

Make it ahead

Brandade will keep in the fridge for a couple of days. Spread in a baking dish, drizzle with olive oil, and heat in a 400°F oven for 20 to 25 minutes before serving.

Serve it with

◆ Toasted baguette slices and fresh tomatoes
◆ Slow-Roasted Tomatoes (page 43)
◆ Roasted Beet and Arugula Salad (page 59)
◆ Salad of Bitter Greens with Asiago (page 60)

Change it up

◆ Spread brandade in a decorative baking dish, drizzle with olive oil, and bake at 400°F until lightly browned, about 20 to 25 minutes. Serve warm, right in the baking dish, with toasted baguette rounds to spread it on.

Spicy Crab Cakes

If you've ever tried to make crab cakes, you know that they're not as easy as they look. It takes forever to form all those patties and coat them in breadcrumbs, and then you have to stand over the stove frying them a few at a time—and to rub salt in the wound, they always fall apart. Not these! Make a quick crumb crust right in a muffin tin, scoop in the crab mixture, top with more crumbs, and pop them in the oven. Toss together a quick side salad while they bake and you'll still have time to enjoy a glass of wine with your guests before dinner. Use either fresh crabmeat or pasteurized crabmeat found in the refrigerator section of your supermarket—don't use the stuff you find on the shelf near the canned tuna! If you can't find mascarpone, substitute regular cream cheese.

¾ cup (6 ounces) mascarpone, at room temperature
3 ounces (about 1 cup) grated Parmesan cheese, divided
1 large egg
1 medium jalapeño chile, stemmed, seeded, and minced
½ teaspoon kosher salt
2 tablespoons (loosely packed) minced cilantro
1 pound crabmeat, broken into small pieces
1½ cups panko (Japanese breadcrumbs)
½ cup (1 stick) unsalted butter

Preheat oven to 350°F. Grease a 12-cup standard muffin tin with softened butter, vegetable or olive oil, or vegetable or olive oil spray.

In a medium bowl, combine mascarpone, ¼ cup grated Parmesan, egg, jalapeño, salt, and cilantro. Stir to mix well. Stir in crabmeat and set aside.

In a saucepan on the stovetop or a medium bowl in the microwave, melt the butter. Add the panko and the remaining ¾ cup Parmesan and mix with a fork until the breadcrumbs are evenly moistened.

Place 1 heaping tablespoon breadcrumb mixture in each of the muffin cups, pressing into the bottom and up the sides to form a crust. Scoop crab mixture into the muffin cups (a standard-sized ice cream scoop works perfectly), dividing equally and pressing down a bit to flatten. Top with another spoonful of the breadcrumb mixture, spreading it out with your fingers to form an even crust.

Bake in preheated oven for 35 to 40 minutes, until the tops are golden brown. Remove pan from oven and let sit about 5 minutes. To remove crab cakes from pan, run a knife around the edge of each cup and carefully lift out. Serve warm.

Makes 12 crab cakes.

Make it ahead

The crab mixture can be made one day ahead and kept, covered, in the fridge. The crab cakes can also be assembled and baked one day ahead. Leave them in the muffin tin, cover, and refrigerate. Heat in preheated 350°F oven about 20 to 25 minutes, or until heated through.

Serve it with

✦ Roasted Beet and Arugula Salad (page 59)
✦ Salad of Bitter Greens with Asiago (page 60)

Change it up

✦ For an appetizer version, use a mini muffin pan to make twice as many smaller cakes and adjust the cooking time accordingly.

Prawns in Romesco Sauce

We love the simplicity of roasting the sauce ingredients together in the oven and then whirling them in a food processor to make the sauce. We simplify the recipe even further by using store-bought roasted red peppers and buying prawns that are already peeled and deveined. Broiling the prawns in the sauce keeps them plump and juicy, and keeps the mess to a minimum. (Note: you can use the same baking dish that you used to roast the sauce ingredients, without having to wash it!)

3 cloves garlic, peeled
¼ cup blanched almonds
2 large Roma tomatoes, quartered lengthwise
½ cup plus 2 tablespoons olive oil, divided
1 teaspoon kosher salt, divided
1 whole roasted red bell pepper (from a jar or roasted fresh and then peeled and seeded)
2 tablespoons red wine vinegar
1 teaspoon smoked or sweet paprika
¼–½ teaspoon cayenne pepper
¼–½ teaspoon freshly ground black pepper
1 pound peeled and deveined medium prawns
8 medium-sized slices crusty bread, such as sourdough batard
2 tablespoons minced fresh flat leaf parsley

Preheat oven to 450° F.

Toss garlic, almonds, and tomatoes with 2 tablespoons olive oil in a broiler-safe dish. Sprinkle with ¼ teaspoon salt and arrange in a single layer. Roast in preheated oven for 10 to 15 minutes, until tomatoes begin to soften and almonds begin to brown.

Transfer to a food processor or blender and add roasted pepper, vinegar, remaining ½ cup olive oil, paprika, cayenne, black pepper, and remaining ¾ teaspoon salt. Process until almonds are ground and mixture is well combined. Taste, and add additional salt, black pepper, or cayenne if needed. If sauce is too thick, add a little more olive oil.

Preheat broiler. In the same dish you used for roasting the tomatoes, toss prawns with sauce, and spread in a single layer. Broil 5 to 10 minutes, until prawns are cooked through and just beginning to brown on top.

While prawns are cooking, toast bread. Arrange 2 slices of toasted bread on each of 4 serving plates.

When prawns are cooked, spoon over bread, dividing equally. Finish by spooning over some of the sauce and garnish with minced parsley.

Serves 4.

Make it ahead

The sauce, not including prawns, can be made a couple of days ahead. Store, covered, in the refrigerator until ready to use. Toss prawns with the sauce and continue following directions.

Serve it with

✦ A simple green salad dressed with Lemon Vinaigrette (page 148) or Sherry-Shallot Vinaigrette (page 150)

Change it up

✦ Substitute Slow-Roasted Tomatoes (page 43) for the Romas, adding them with the roasted pepper, vinegar, and spices.

Pasta with Asparagus, Leeks, and Chèvre

This gorgeous pasta dish is the picture of spring. Creamy, tangy goat cheese serves as the perfect backdrop for pale and dark green asparagus disks, pale green leeks, and flecks of bright yellow lemon zest. For quick preparation and easy cleanup, roast the asparagus and leeks while you boil the pasta, and toss the sauce together in the same pot.

2 pounds asparagus, woody ends snapped off, sliced on a sharp diagonal into ⅛-inch-thick disks
2 medium leeks (white and pale green part only), trimmed, halved lengthwise, and thinly sliced
2 tablespoons olive oil or olive oil spray
1 teaspoon kosher salt
½–1 teaspoon freshly ground black pepper
1 pound dry pasta (gemelli, fusilli, rotelle, cavatappi, orecchiette, or other short pasta)
5 ounces chèvre, cut into a few pieces
½ cup half-and-half or heavy cream
grated zest of one lemon, preferably Meyer
3 tablespoons lemon juice (from about 1 lemon, preferably Meyer)
freshly grated Parmesan cheese for serving (optional)

Preheat oven to 450°F.

Set a large pot of salted water (large enough to hold all ingredients) over high heat to boil for pasta.

Place asparagus and leeks on a large rimmed baking sheet, toss or spray with olive oil, and sprinkle with salt and pepper. Roast in preheated oven until asparagus is tender, about 10 minutes.

While the vegetables are roasting, cook pasta according to the instructions on the package. When pasta is done, reserve 1 cup of the cooking water and drain pasta in a colander. Place pasta pot back on the stove over medium heat. Add chèvre and half-and-half or cream and cook, stirring frequently, until the cheese is melted. Stir in lemon zest and juice. Add asparagus, leeks, and pasta and stir until well combined. If you like a creamier consistency, add a little of the reserved pasta water or more half-and-half or cream. Taste, and add additional salt and pepper if needed. Serve immediately, garnished with freshly grated Parmesan, if desired.

Serves 6 to 8.

Make it ahead

The asparagus and leeks can be roasted up to one day ahead. Store, covered, in the fridge until ready to add to the sauce.

Serve it with

✦ Crusty bread

✦ Simple salad of baby greens dressed with Lemon Vinaigrette (page 148)

Change it up

✦ Substitute 2 pounds of thawed frozen quartered artichoke hearts for the asparagus. Artichoke hearts don't need to be roasted, so instead, after draining the pasta, return the pot to the stove and heat olive oil in it over medium-high heat. Sauté leeks in the oil until soft, about 3 to 5 minutes, add the artichoke hearts, and cook, stirring, until heated through. Reduce heat to medium and stir in cheese and cream. Cook until cheese is melted, about 2 minutes, and stir in lemon zest and juice. Serve topped with grated Parmesan cheese and chopped Kalamata olives.

Gemelli with Roasted Cauliflower, Tomatoes, and Crispy Breadcrumbs

Roasting the cauliflower with red onions and garlic brings out the sweet, earthy flavors. Plus, you can prepare the rest of the dish while the vegetables are in the oven. Feel free to substitute another pasta shape—rotelle, orecchiette, or small shells would work well—if your supermarket doesn't carry gemelli.

1 head cauliflower (about 1½ pounds florets), cut into small pieces
1 small red onion, thinly sliced
2 cloves garlic, thinly sliced
2–3 tablespoons olive oil
1 teaspoon kosher salt
½–1 teaspoon freshly ground black pepper
¾ pound gemelli or other pasta
4 cups (about 6 ounces) sourdough bread cubes
4 tablespoons (½ stick) unsalted butter
1 28-ounce can diced tomatoes, drained (reserve juice)
¼ cup capers, drained
¼–1 teaspoon crushed red pepper
freshly grated Parmesan cheese for serving

Preheat oven to 450°F.

In a baking dish, toss cauliflower, onion, and garlic with olive oil, coating vegetables thoroughly. Season with salt and pepper, and roast in preheated oven for 35 to 45 minutes, stirring once about halfway through, until cauliflower is tender and beginning to brown.

While the vegetables are in the oven, heat a large pot of salted water (large enough to hold all ingredients) over high heat and cook pasta according to the instructions on the package.

Whirl bread in a food processor to make crumbs, pulsing, until the largest pieces are roughly the size of peas. Heat a large, heavy skillet over medium-high heat and add butter. When butter is melted and bubbling, add the breadcrumbs and cook, stirring frequently, until crispy, about 8 to 10 minutes. Remove from heat and set aside.

When pasta is cooked, drain and return to the pot on the stove. Add roasted vegetables, tomatoes, capers, and crushed red pepper and cook over medium heat, stirring, until just heated through. If the mixture looks too dry, add a bit of the reserved tomato juice. Stir until well combined. Serve in pasta bowls topped with breadcrumbs and generously garnished with cheese.

Serves 6 to 8.

Make it ahead

Breadcrumbs can be toasted a few days ahead and stored, covered, in the fridge. When ready to use, let sit out on the counter until warmed to room temperature.

Serve it with

✦ Spring Leek, Pea, and Lettuce Soup (page 73)

Pasta with Butternut Squash and Crispy Fried Sage Leaves

This pasta's secret ingredient, ricotta salata, is nothing like the moist, spoonable ricotta cheese most of us are familiar with. This ricotta (which simply means "recooked" in Italian) is a firm, mild, salted sheep's milk cheese that makes a tasty addition to pastas and salads. If you have trouble finding it, crumbled feta would be a good substitute. By the way, precubed butternut squash is available in many supermarkets, and as you could have guessed, we approve of using it. You should also feel free to substitute a handful of minced fresh sage leaves if you're not up for frying them.

4 cups (about 1½ pounds) peeled and cubed butternut squash
3 tablespoons olive oil
½ teaspoon kosher salt
¼–½ teaspoon cayenne pepper
12 ounces cavatappi or other pasta
3 tablespoons unsalted butter, cut into small pieces
4 ounces (about 1 cup) crumbled or grated ricotta salata cheese
1¼ cups toasted pecan halves
Crispy Fried Sage Leaves (page 160)

Preheat oven to 400°F.

In a large baking dish toss squash, olive oil, salt, and cayenne until squash is thoroughly coated. Spread in a single layer and bake in preheated oven 30 to 40 minutes, stirring occasionally, until squash is soft.

While squash is roasting, cook pasta according to the instructions on the package. Crumble or grate the cheese. When pasta is cooked, drain it well and put in a large serving bowl. Add the butter to the hot pasta and toss until butter is melted. Add roasted squash, cheese, and pecans and toss to combine. Sprinkle fried sage leaves on top. Serve warm.

Serves 4 to 6.

Serve it with

✦ A crisp green salad with Lemon Vinaigrette (page 148) or Sherry-Shallot Vinaigrette (page 150)

Change it up

✦ Substitute grated Parmesan or crumbled feta for the ricotta salata.
✦ Substitute a tablespoon or two of minced fresh sage for the fried sage leaves, stirring it in with the cheese.

Roasted Salmon with Garlic Confit

Savory and sweet roasted garlic smothers this simple salmon dish with deliciousness.

1 head of Roasted Garlic (page 162)
1 teaspoon salt, divided
½–1 teaspoon freshly ground black pepper, divided
1 tablespoon minced fresh rosemary or oregano
2 tablespoons olive oil
3 tablespoons lemon juice (from about 1 lemon)
4 6-ounce salmon fillets (about 1 inch thick)

Preheat oven to 450°F.

When roasted garlic is cool enough to handle, squeeze cloves out of their skins into a small bowl. Add ½ teaspoon salt, ¼ to ½ teaspoon pepper, and rosemary or oregano, and mash to a paste with a fork. Add olive oil and lemon juice and stir to combine.

Place salmon on a baking sheet, season with remaining salt and pepper, and spread the garlic confit over the fillets, dividing evenly. Bake salmon, uncovered, in preheated oven until cooked through (15 to 20 minutes). Serve immediately.

Serves 4.

Make it ahead

The garlic confit can be made a day or so ahead and stored, covered, in the fridge.

Serve it with
+ Spiced Chard with Quinoa and Currants (page 140)
+ Quinoa Pilaf with Brussels Sprouts and Carrots (page 142)
+ Cumin-Raisin Couscous (page 144)
+ Plain white or brown rice or couscous and sautéed chard

Moroccan Chickpea Stew with Charmoula

Vegetarians and meat-eaters alike adore this hearty bean and vegetable stew. The magic ingredient is our to-die-for Charmoula (page 155), which adds intense flavor and depth.

2 tablespoons unsalted butter
2 tablespoons olive oil
1 medium red onion, diced
2 cloves garlic, minced
½ cup dry white wine
1 15-ounce can garbanzo beans (chickpeas), rinsed and drained
2 medium carrots, peeled and diced or cut into coins
1 medium turnip, diced
1 teaspoon kosher salt
1 teaspoon smoked or sweet paprika
1 teaspoon ground cumin
½ teaspoon ground coriander
2 cups water
1–2 teaspoons chile paste or ¼–½ teaspoon cayenne pepper, or to taste
6 cups (packed) baby spinach (about 8 ounces)
¼ cup plain, whole-milk yogurt
Charmoula (page 155)

In a stockpot, heat butter and olive oil over medium-high heat until butter is melted and bubbling. Add onions and garlic and cook, stirring frequently, until onions are softened, about 3 minutes. Add wine, chickpeas, carrots, turnips, salt, paprika, cumin, coriander, and water. Return heat to medium-high and bring to a boil. Reduce heat to medium-low and simmer, uncovered, until vegetables are soft, about 20 minutes.

When the vegetables are soft, stir chile paste and spinach into the stew and continue to cook until spinach is wilted, about 2 minutes. Taste, and add additional salt if needed. Stir in yogurt. Ladle stew into bowls, top each with a heaping tablespoon of charmoula, and serve immediately.

Serves 4 to 6.

Make it ahead

The stew can be made a couple of days ahead up to and including the 20 minutes of simmering. Store, covered, in the fridge until ready to serve. Before serving, reheat over medium heat until warmed, and continue following instructions.

Serve it with
+ A crisp green salad with Sherry-Shallot Vinaigrette (page 150)
+ Steamed brown or white rice

Lemon-Herb Salt-Baked Trout

The trout is baked in a thick crust of salt, which solidifies as it cooks. Be sure to gather your guests around to watch as you crack the shell, revealing the moist and delicious fish inside. As an added bonus, if your party is boring, this unusual cooking method will give your guests something to talk about.

4 whole river trout, about 8 ounces each, butterflied and deboned (ask your fish dealer to do this for you)
2 Meyer lemons, sliced paper thin
1 tablespoon fresh thyme leaves
2 tablespoons unsalted butter, cut into small pieces
1 3-pound box kosher salt
⅓ cup water

Preheat oven to 450°F.

With the trout open like books on your work surface, layer the lemon slices, thyme leaves, and butter on them, dividing evenly. Close up each fish securely, so the insides don't fill up with salt in the next step. If they're not closing cooperatively, use a toothpick or two.

Line a baking dish with aluminum foil and add a layer of salt ½ inch thick. Place stuffed trout on salt and cover with more salt—so that the fish is encased in ½ inch of salt all the way around. Sprinkle with water. Bake in preheated oven for 10 to 20 minutes (depending on the size of the fish) until fish is firm to the touch. When finished, salt will have formed a hard crust that can be cracked right off. Break all the hardened salt off carefully and discard. (Don't serve any of the salt with the fish.) Serve the fish with the skin on, but advise the diners not to eat it.

Serves 4.

Serve it with
+ Butter-Braised Radishes (page 132)
+ Shredded Brussels Sprouts with Horseradish Cream (page 138)
+ Any mixed green salad

Black Cod en Papillote with Fennel, Baby Spinach, and Olives

En papillote is French for "cooked in a paper bag"—the bag made of parchment paper, which you'll find at just about any supermarket, near the waxed paper. This cooking method allows you to cook the fish and veggies together while sealing in all the flavors of the dish—and it makes for easy cleanup, too. Delivering a puffed-up, steamy paper packet for each diner to unwrap makes this dish seem extra special. Crisp, aromatic fennel balances the strong, salty flavor of olives and keeps the fish moist while it cooks. Currants and lemon zest add surprising sweet and tangy notes to the dish.

¼ cup currants
½ cup sliced Kalamata olives
2 cloves garlic, minced
2 tablespoons capers, drained
¼–½ teaspoon crushed red pepper
grated zest of 1 lemon
2 tablespoons olive oil
¼ cup dry white wine
½ teaspoon kosher salt
½ teaspoon freshly ground black pepper
4 cups (loosely packed) baby spinach leaves
1 medium fennel bulb, cored and very thinly sliced (leafy tops discarded)
4 6-ounce black cod fillets
8 fresh thyme sprigs

Preheat oven to 400°F.

In a small bowl combine currants, olives, garlic, capers, crushed red pepper, lemon zest, olive oil, wine, salt, and pepper.

Cut four 15 x 15-inch squares of parchment paper and spray or drizzle with olive oil. Divide the spinach and fennel evenly by handfuls among the four parchment squares. Top vegetables with cod fillets. Spoon a quarter of the olive mixture (including the liquid) over each fish fillet, and top each with 2 thyme sprigs.

To seal packets, bring two opposite edges of the parchment paper together above the filling and fold over about 1 inch, making a crease. If you've got enough paper, fold over one or two more times in the same manner, being sure to leave some room in the packet for steam to build up and circulate. Fold and crimp the open ends together to seal the packet on both ends. Place parchment packets on a baking sheet and cook in preheated oven, 15 to 18 minutes (depending on the thickness of the fish), until cooked through.

Serve the fish on serving plates in their packets, or place each packet in a wide, flat pasta bowl, open it, and slide the contents, including the juice, out into the bowl, and serve.

Serves 4.

Make it ahead

The packets can be assembled and stored in the fridge several hours ahead.

Serve it with

✦ Cumin-Raisin Couscous (page 144)

✦ Steamed rice or plain couscous

Change it up

✦ If black cod (also called sablefish or butterfish) isn't available, feel free to substitute any firm white fish such as halibut, sole, or swordfish.

Mussels Steamed in Spicy Fennel and Saffron Broth

The herby, seafood-infused scent of this broth will instantly transport you to a sunny, warm afternoon in a sidewalk café in the south of France. To complete the experience, pair this dish with a dry French rosé.

2 tablespoons olive oil
1 medium red onion, thinly sliced
4 cloves garlic, minced
2 medium fennel bulbs, cored and thinly sliced (leafy tops discarded or saved for another use)
1 teaspoon kosher salt
½–1 teaspoon crushed red pepper, or to taste
1 cup dry white wine
1 cup canned diced tomatoes, drained
2 cups clam juice or fish broth
pinch of saffron
2 pounds mussels, rinsed and debearded (discard any that are open prior to cooking)
¼ cup (loosely packed) minced flat leaf parsley

In a large stockpot, heat the oil over medium-high heat until hot but not smoking. Add the onions, garlic, and fennel and cook, stirring occasionally, until vegetables soften, about 5 minutes. Add salt, crushed red pepper, and wine and cook, stirring occasionally, about 3 minutes more. Add tomatoes and clam juice or fish broth and bring to a boil. Stir in saffron and add mussels. Cover and simmer 5 to 10 minutes, until the mussels have opened. (Discard any that haven't opened after 10 minutes of cooking.) To serve, ladle mussels, vegetables, and broth into bowls and garnish with parsley.

Serves 4 to 6.

Make it ahead

The broth can be made a day or two ahead up to and including adding the tomatoes and clam juice. Store, covered, in the refrigerator until ready to use. Bring to a boil before adding mussels, and continue with the rest of the instructions.

Serve it with

✦ Lots of crusty bread for dipping
✦ Mixed green salad with a light vinaigrette

Change it up

✦ Replace the mussels with small clams, such as Manila, or a meaty white fish such as cod or halibut.

✦ For more depth of flavor, add a diced Spanish chorizo sausage with the onions, garlic, and fennel.

Top Sirloin with Charmoula on a Bed of Arugula

If you haven't yet been introduced to the magic of charmoula—a North African condiment packed with herbs, chiles, garlic, and lemon—we urge you not to wait a moment longer. Dolloped onto individually plated sliced steak atop a bed of bright green arugula, this dish will impress your guests before they even taste it. And top sirloin is an affordable cut of beef so tender that it doesn't require marinating, making this simple dish one step easier.

½ teaspoon kosher salt
½ teaspoon freshly ground black pepper
2 tablespoons olive oil
2 12-ounce boneless top sirloin steaks, about 1 inch thick
4 cups (loosely packed) arugula
⅔ cup Charmoula (page 155)

Preheat oven to 350°F (optional).

Sprinkle both sides of steak evenly with salt and pepper. Heat oil in a heavy skillet over medium-high heat until hot but not smoking, and cook steaks 4 to 6 minutes on each side for medium-rare. If you like your steaks more well done, transfer them to preheated oven until done to your preference. Let rest for 5 minutes before slicing.

Slice steak across the grain into ¼-inch slices. Divide arugula evenly among 4 plates, lay steak slices on the arugula, and top with a dollop of charmoula.

Serves 4.

Serve it with

✦ Cumin-Raisin Couscous (page 144)
✦ Spiced Chard with Quinoa and Currants (page 140)
✦ Rice, Barley, Lentil, and Mushroom Pilaf (page 146)

Seared Sea Scallops with Mint and Pea Purée

There's something about seared scallops that seems so special and fancy (maybe it's the price?) yet they're not especially difficult to make. Set on a bed of bright green mint and pea purée, they look absolutely regal.

4 tablespoons olive oil, divided
1 medium shallot, minced
2 cloves garlic, minced
¾ cup fish, chicken, or vegetable broth or water
2 cups (about 10 ounces) fresh or frozen peas
¼ cup (lightly packed) fresh mint leaves, plus more, julienned, for garnish
½ cup sour cream
½ teaspoon kosher salt, plus more for seasoning scallops
¼–½ teaspoon freshly ground black pepper
3 tablespoons fresh lemon juice (juice of about 1 lemon)
16 large sea scallops (about 1½ pounds), rinsed and patted dry

In a medium saucepan, heat 2 tablespoons olive oil over medium-high heat until hot but not smoking. Add shallot and garlic and sauté until shallot is soft and translucent, about 3 minutes. Add broth and bring to a boil. Add peas and return to a boil, reduce heat to medium-low, and simmer until peas are tender, about 5 minutes. Stir in mint, sour cream, salt, pepper, and lemon juice. Using an immersion blender (or in batches in a countertop blender or food processor), purée until smooth. Taste, and add additional salt and pepper if needed.

In a large, heavy skillet, heat remaining 2 tablespoons olive oil over medium-high heat. When oil is hot but not smoking, place scallops in the pan, making sure they are not touching each other. Cook 2 to 3 minutes, without moving them around, until the bottoms form a crisp, caramel-colored crust. Turn and cook the other sides the same way. Scallops are done when they feel springy, but not overly firm, to the touch.

Reheat the pea purée in the saucepan over medium-low heat and add a touch more broth or water if it is too thick. Spoon onto four serving plates and arrange the scallops on top. Sprinkle with a little julienned mint.

Serves 4.

Make it ahead

The purée can be made a couple of days ahead and stored, covered, in the fridge. Reheat in a saucepan before serving.

Serve it with

+ Crusty bread for sopping up the rich, creamy purée

Change it up

+ Drizzle a bit of truffle oil over just before serving.
+ Crumble crispy bacon on top before serving.
+ Substitute baked, broiled, or grilled shrimp or salmon for the scallops.
+ Add a few additional cups of broth and serve, garnished with shredded Parmesan cheese and crunchy croutons, as a refreshing soup.

Chicken with Lemon and Olives

We love a party-worthy dish that can be prepped in under 10 minutes and then popped into the oven for the better part of an hour, giving us plenty of time to ready ourselves for the festivities.

grated zest of one lemon
6 tablespoons lemon juice (from about 2 lemons)
¼ cup dry white wine
2 tablespoons olive oil
¼–½ teaspoon crushed red pepper, or to taste
1 teaspoon kosher salt
¼–½ teaspoon freshly ground black pepper
1 tablespoon capers, with some of the juice
2 tablespoons chopped fresh oregano or 2 teaspoons dried oregano
4 cloves garlic, minced
1 whole chicken (about 3½ pounds), cut into pieces, or 6 thighs
1 cup sliced Kalamata olives

Preheat oven to 400°F.

In a small bowl combine the lemon zest and juice, wine, olive oil, crushed red pepper, salt, black pepper, capers, oregano, and garlic. Place the chicken in a baking dish in a single layer and pour the lemon juice mixture over it. Scatter olives over and around the chicken pieces. Bake, uncovered, in preheated oven about 50 minutes, until chicken is browned on top and cooked through.

Serves 4 to 6.

Make it ahead

The chicken can be marinated in the lemon juice mixture for up to 24 hours, covered, in the refrigerator. Remove the baking dish from the fridge about 45 minutes before cooking, allow the chicken to come to room temperature, and proceed with the recipe.

Serve it with

✦ Quinoa Pilaf with Brussels Sprouts and Carrots (page 142)
✦ Spiced Chard with Quinoa and Currants (page 140)
✦ Rice, Barley, Lentil, and Mushroom Pilaf (page 146)

Change it up

✦ Use any fresh or dried herb in place of the oregano, such as rosemary, thyme, or basil, or a combination.

Pomegranate-Roasted Chicken with Figs and Ginger

This simple recipe uses bottled pomegranate juice, which can be found in just about any supermarket these days, eliminating the hassle and mess of seeding pomegranates yourself. The pomegranate juice serves to tenderize the chicken as it marinates and then turns into a thick, gingery sauce as the chicken cooks.

1 whole chicken (about 3½ pounds), cut into pieces, or 6 thighs
1 medium onion, quartered and thinly sliced
1 cup pomegranate juice
¼ cup dry red wine
¼ cup (packed) brown sugar
2 tablespoons olive oil
3 tablespoons minced fresh ginger
1½ teaspoons kosher salt
½–1 teaspoon freshly ground black pepper
6 ounces (about 1 cup) dried figs, stemmed and halved or quartered, depending on size
⅓ cup toasted crushed walnuts

Arrange the chicken pieces, skin side up, in a single layer in a baking dish and scatter the sliced onions over the top. In a small bowl, combine the pomegranate juice, wine, brown sugar, olive oil, ginger, salt, and pepper. Pour marinade over the chicken pieces, turning to coat. Cover and refrigerate at least 1 hour or overnight.

Preheat oven to 450°F.

Add figs to chicken, stirring a bit to make sure figs are moistened by the marinade. Roast chicken, uncovered, in preheated oven for 50 to 60 minutes, basting occasionally, until cooked through. Remove from oven and sprinkle with crushed walnuts. Serve hot with some of the sauce, figs, and onions spooned over the top.

Serve it with
+ Farro with Peas and Radishes (page 141)
+ Rice, Barley, Lentil, and Mushroom Pilaf (page 146)
+ Brown rice and sautéed chard

Change it up
+ Sprinkle a couple of handfuls of fresh pomegranate seeds over the chicken before serving.

Chicken with Coconut Milk, Chiles, and Basil

Rich coconut milk gets a lift from spicy fresh chiles and sprightly basil, making this simple sauce taste truly luxurious. We love the method of sticking the chicken in the oven to roast while you make the quick sauce on the stovetop.

1 whole chicken (about 3½ pounds), cut into pieces, or 6 thighs
3 tablespoons vegetable oil, divided
½ teaspoon kosher salt
¼–½ teaspoon freshly ground black pepper
1 medium shallot, minced
1 tablespoon minced fresh ginger
1 14-ounce can unsweetened coconut milk
1 tablespoon brown sugar
1–2 jalapeño or serrano chiles, seeded and minced
2 tablespoons fish sauce or light soy sauce
2 tablespoons lime juice (from about 1½ limes)
⅓ cup (tightly packed) minced fresh basil
1–2 red jalapeño chiles, or 1 small red bell pepper, stemmed, seeded, and finely diced, for garnish

Preheat oven to 425°F.

Trim any excess fatty skin off the chicken, if needed. Place chicken in a single layer in a large baking dish and coat with 1 tablespoon vegetable oil and season with salt and pepper. Roast in preheated oven for 30 minutes.

While chicken is roasting, make the sauce. Heat remaining 2 tablespoons of vegetable oil in a large skillet over medium-high heat. Add shallots and ginger and cook, stirring, until shallot is soft and translucent, about 3 minutes. Add coconut milk, brown sugar, chiles, and fish sauce or soy sauce and bring to a boil. Reduce heat to medium and simmer until sauce thickens, 10 to 15 minutes. Stir in lime juice and basil and remove from heat.

When chicken has roasted for 30 minutes, remove from oven and pour sauce over the chicken pieces. Return chicken to the oven and roast about 15 minutes more, until chicken is fully cooked. Serve garnished with diced red jalapeño or red bell pepper.

Make it ahead

The sauce can be made a couple of days ahead and kept, covered, in the fridge. Reheat briefly in the microwave or on the stovetop before adding to hot chicken.

Serve it with

✦ Coconut Rice (page 145) or plain steamed rice

✦ Green beans sautéed with garlic

Change it up

✦ Replace the whole chicken with 6 or 8 duck legs. Season the legs with salt and pepper (leave out the vegetable oil) and roast in a 375ºF oven for 1 hour. Drain the fat from the pan. (The easiest way to do this is to transfer the duck legs to a plate using tongs, pour off the fat, and return the duck legs to the pan.) Add ¼ cup chicken broth or water to the sauce to thin it a bit, if needed, and pour it over the duck legs in the baking dish. Return the duck to the oven and roast for 30 minutes more, until the meat is cooked through.

Spicy Chicken Mole

Mexican mole sauces are complex mixtures of ground spices and nuts, often with deep, dark chocolate. Making the real deal can take literally days of laborious toasting, chopping, and grinding. This immensely simplified version may be more involved than many of our other recipes, but we're pretty sure the adoration it will earn you from your guests is well worth the effort. Bonus: you can tell them you've been toiling over it for weeks—and they'll believe you!

        3 tablespoons vegetable oil, divided
        1 large onion, diced
        4 cloves garlic, minced
        2 tablespoons all-purpose flour
        1 teaspoon ground coriander
        1 teaspoon ground cumin
        1 tablespoon (mild) chili powder
        ½ teaspoon ground cinnamon
        1½ teaspoons kosher salt, divided
        1–2 whole chipotle chiles, to taste, from a can of *chipotles en adobo*,
            plus 1–2 tablespoons adobo sauce
        2 ounces semisweet baking chocolate, chopped
        3 tablespoons creamy peanut butter
        1 cup canned diced tomatoes with green chiles (or 1 cup canned diced tomatoes
            and 1 tablespoon canned diced green chiles)
        ¼ cup raisins
        2–3 cups chicken broth
        1 whole chicken (about 3½ pounds), cut into pieces, or 6 thighs
        ¼ cup chopped cilantro for garnish

Preheat oven to 425°F.

Heat 2 tablespoons oil in a large skillet over medium-high heat. When oil is hot but not smoking, add onions and garlic and sauté until onions are soft and translucent, about 5 to 7 minutes. Sprinkle flour over the onions and cook, stirring, about 2 minutes, until flour is incorporated and just beginning to brown. Add coriander, cumin, chili powder, cinnamon, and 1 teaspoon salt. Give the spices a stir and add the chipotle chile(s) with adobo sauce, chocolate, peanut butter, tomatoes, raisins, and 2 cups broth. Bring to a boil, reduce heat to medium, and simmer, uncovered, stirring occasionally, about 45 minutes.

While sauce is simmering, trim any excess fatty skin off the chicken, if needed. Place chicken in a single layer in a large baking dish, coat with the remaining 1 tablespoon vegetable oil, and season with the remaining ½ teaspoon of salt. Roast in preheated oven for 30 minutes.

When sauce has been simmering about 45 minutes, purée using an immersion blender (or in batches in a countertop blender or food processor), until smooth. The sauce should be about the consistency of thick tomato sauce. If it's too thick, add a bit more broth as needed.

When chicken has roasted for 30 minutes and the sauce has been puréed, remove chicken from oven and pour sauce over the chicken pieces. Chicken pieces should be coated with sauce and the sauce should come about halfway up the chicken pieces. Reserve any remaining sauce for serving. Return the chicken to the oven and roast 15 minutes more, until sauce is bubbly and chicken is fully cooked.

Transfer the chicken pieces to a serving platter or individual serving plates, drizzle the sauce over the top, scatter cilantro over, and serve.

Serves 4 to 6.

Make it ahead

The sauce can be made a few days ahead and kept, covered, in the fridge. Bring it to room temperature or heat it gently on the stove before pouring it over the hot chicken. Leftover Spicy Chicken Mole can be made into mouthwatering enchiladas: shred the meat for the filling, roll up in corn tortillas, smother with mole sauce, top with grated cheese, and bake in a 350°F oven until hot and bubbly.

Serve it with

+ Farro with Peas and Radishes (page 141)
+ White or brown rice or warm tortillas
+ Garlicky sautéed chard

Change it up

+ Replace the whole chicken or thighs with 6 or 8 duck legs. Place them in a single layer in a large baking dish and season with salt and pepper. Roast in preheated (375°F) oven for an hour. Pour off the fat. (Remove the duck legs to a platter, pour the fat out of the baking dish, and return the duck legs to the baking dish.) Add ½ cup or so of broth to the sauce to thin it a bit and return to the oven and roast about 30 minutes more, until duck is fully cooked.
+ Forget about poultry altogether, and try mole sauce on oven-roasted potatoes or other vegetables, or served over brown rice.

Moroccan-Spiced Cornish Game Hens with Lemon and Mint

Serving half a small bird per person makes for a stunning presentation. The vivid Moroccan flavors of the butter give roast poultry an exotic new meaning. (Note: you could use just about any of our compound butters in this recipe.) Preparation is a snap—the butter can even be made well ahead and smeared on the birds while the oven preheats.

> 2 Cornish game hens (about 2 pounds each)
> ½ teaspoon kosher salt
> ¼–½ teaspoon freshly ground black pepper
> ½ recipe Moroccan Spiced Butter (page 153), at room temperature
> 2 cups chicken broth

Preheat oven to 400°F.

Rinse the hens under running water and pat dry. Slide your fingers under the skin of the breast of each hen to loosen it. Season each inside and out with salt and pepper. Spread 1 tablespoon butter under the skin of each hen, spread another teaspoon or so over the outside of each hen, and place about 1 teaspoon butter inside each cavity.

Place hens on a roasting rack, breast up, in large roasting pan. Pour ½ cup broth over hens and roast in preheated oven for a total of about 60 minutes. Baste 2 or 3 times during the first 30 minutes, each time adding another ½ cup of broth and spreading a little of the remaining butter onto the hens, until all the broth and butter is used up. When hens are cooked through (the juice should run clear when pierced in the thickest part of the thigh), remove them from oven, cover loosely with foil, and let rest for 5 minutes. If desired, cut each hen in half using a large chef's knife or cleaver, and serve immediately with the pan juices in a gravy boat or drizzled right over the hens.

Serves 2 to 4.

Serve it with
- ✦ Spiced Chard with Quinoa and Currants (page 140)
- ✦ Cumin-Raisin Couscous (page 144)
- ✦ Any hearty greens such as kale or chard, sautéed with garlic

Change it up
- ✦ Try it with Garlic-Herb Butter, Chipotle-Honey Butter, or any of our other Compound Butters (page 153) in place of the Moroccan Spiced Butter.

Lamb Burgers with Feta Cheese and Charmoula

Lamb, feta, and charmoula—a spicy North African condiment made with fresh herbs and dried spices—take a traditional American dish in an unexpected direction. We can pretty much guarantee that these burgers will make you the star of any barbecue, but they're great cooked in a skillet on the stove, too.

1¼ pounds ground lamb
½ cup chopped onion
4 ounces (about ¾ cup) crumbled feta cheese
¾ teaspoon kosher salt
¼–½ teaspoon freshly ground black pepper
2 tablespoons vegetable oil (if cooking on stovetop)
1 medium tomato, sliced
½ cup Charmoula (page 155)
4 good-quality hamburger buns or sandwich rolls, toasted

In a large mixing bowl, thoroughly mix lamb, onion, feta, salt, and pepper. Form mixture into 4 patties. If cooking on the stove, heat vegetable oil over medium-high heat until hot but not smoking, or simply heat a barbecue to medium-high, and cook burgers about 5 minutes per side for medium (or shorter or longer to achieve desired doneness).

Divide burgers, tomato slices, and charmoula evenly among the 4 buns.

Makes 4 burgers.

Make it ahead

The lamb patties can be formed and stored, wrapped in plastic, in the fridge for several hours prior to cooking.

Serve it with

+ Roasted Beet and Arugula Salad (page 59)
+ Salad of Bitter Greens with Asiago (page 60)
+ Any simple mixed green salad with vinaigrette dressing

Change it up

+ Instead of 4 full-sized burgers, make 12 small "sliders" and serve them on mini hamburger buns.
+ Instead of charmoula, serve with Spiced Yogurt-Cilantro Sauce (page 157), Raita (page 44), mint jelly, or any variety of chutney.

Duck Legs in Port Reduction

Most of us think of duck as one of those things best left to restaurant chefs, but this method—using only the legs, which are the moistest and most flavorful part of the bird—is simple and virtually foolproof. If you don't want to spring for a bottle of port, feel free to substitute a good-quality, big red wine, such as Cabernet Sauvignon or Zinfandel. For a restaurant-worthy plate, serve the duck over our Baked Polenta with Mascarpone and Corn (page 143).

6 large duck legs, 8 to 10 ounces each, trimmed of excess fat
grated zest of 1 orange
1½ teaspoons kosher salt, divided
¼–½ teaspoon freshly ground black pepper
2 tablespoons olive oil
1 medium onion, diced
1 medium bulb fennel, cored and diced
1 medium carrot, peeled and diced
6 fresh thyme sprigs
1 bay leaf
2 tablespoons balsamic vinegar
2 cups port
3 cups chicken broth
2 tablespoons (loosely packed) minced flat leaf parsley

Preheat oven to 375°F.

Place duck legs in an ovenproof baking dish large enough to hold them snugly in a single layer. Sprinkle orange zest, pepper, and ½ teaspoon salt over duck. Roast in preheated oven, uncovered, for 1 hour.

While the duck is in the oven, make the sauce. Heat olive oil in a large skillet over medium-high heat. Add onion, fennel, carrot, thyme sprigs, bay leaf, and the remaining 1 teaspoon salt. Cook, stirring frequently, until vegetables are soft and beginning to brown, about 10 minutes. Add vinegar and port and increase heat to high. Bring the liquid to a boil and cook until it is reduced by half, about 6 to 8 minutes. Add chicken broth and return to a boil. Reduce heat to low and simmer until sauce thickens, 10 to 15 minutes. Remove from heat and set aside.

When duck has been in the oven for an hour, remove the baking dish, leaving the oven on. Drain the fat from the pan. (The easiest way to do this is to transfer the duck legs to a plate using tongs, pour off the fat, and return the duck legs to the dish.) Pour the sauce over the duck legs. The sauce should come about halfway up the duck legs. If you have too much sauce, reserve the extra for serving. (Heat it up and, if desired, reduce it further on the stove.) Return the duck to the oven and roast for 30 minutes more, until the skin is crisp and the meat is cooked through.

Transfer the duck legs to a serving platter or individual serving plates, drizzle the remaining sauce over the top, scatter parsley over, and serve.

Serves 4 to 6.

Make it ahead

The sauce can be made a couple of days ahead and kept, covered, in the fridge. Warm briefly in the microwave or on the stovetop before pouring over hot duck legs.

Serve it with

✦ Baked Polenta with Mascarpone and Corn (page 143)

✦ Cumin-Raisin Couscous (page 144)

✦ Quinoa Pilaf with Brussels Sprouts and Carrots (page 142)

✦ A crisp green salad with Sherry-Shallot Vinaigrette (page 150)

✦ A bold red wine, such as Cabernet Sauvignon, Zinfandel, or Syrah

Five-Spice Roast Pork

Chinese five-spice powder is a combination of cinnamon, cloves, star anise, fennel, and Szechuan peppercorns. Here it infuses the meat with exotic flavor and makes a luxurious reduction to drizzle over the finished dish.

> 1 teaspoon kosher salt, plus a pinch or two for seasoning the meat
> 1 2-pound boneless pork roast (loin or shoulder)
> 3 cloves garlic, minced
> 1 cup port or red wine
> ¼ cup (packed) brown sugar
> 2 tablespoons soy sauce
> 1 tablespoon Chinese five-spice powder
> 1–2 teaspoons Asian chile paste or ¼–½ teaspoon cayenne pepper
> 2 tablespoons vegetable oil

Sprinkle a pinch or two of salt over the meat, seasoning it on all sides.

In a bowl large enough to hold the roast, combine the garlic, port or wine, brown sugar, soy sauce, five-spice powder, chile paste or cayenne, and the remaining 1 teaspoon salt. Stir to combine. Add pork and turn to coat. Cover and refrigerate at least 4 hours or overnight.

Preheat oven to 375°F.

Heat vegetable oil in a large skillet over medium-high heat. When oil is very hot but not smoking, remove roast from marinade (reserving the marinade) and sear it in the hot pan, turning every 2 or 3 minutes, until browned on all sides. Place the browned roast in a baking dish or roasting pan, drizzle about 2 tablespoons marinade over the meat, and place in preheated oven. Cook 15 minutes, turn the roast over, and drizzle with a little more of the marinade. Roast another 30 minutes, or until meat is cooked to desired doneness (about 150°F on a meat thermometer; temperature will increase by another 5 to 10 degrees as the roast rests).

While meat is roasting, pour reserved marinade into the skillet used to brown the meat (there's no need to clean the pan) and bring to a boil. Reduce heat to medium-low and simmer to thicken sauce, 5 to 10 minutes.

When meat is finished cooking, remove from the oven, cover loosely with foil, and let stand 5 to 10 minutes. Slice into ⅛-inch-thick slices and serve with reduced marinade spooned over the top.

Serves 4 to 6.

Make it ahead

The roast can marinate in the refrigerator for up to 48 hours.

Serve it with

✦ Coconut Rice (page 145)

✦ Green beans sautéed with lots of garlic

Change it up

✦ For a more Western flavor, replace the five-spice powder in the marinade with the same amount of dry mustard.

Pistachio-Crusted Roast Leg of Lamb with Spiced Yogurt-Cilantro Sauce

This is a perfect dinner party dish: make the marinade the day before, marinate the meat overnight, and on the day of your party all you have to do is mix up the nut topping (while the oven preheats), coat the meat, and pop it in the oven. Best of all, your sauce is already made, and while the meat is roasting you'll have plenty of time to prepare your side dishes (or run around tidying up your house). The yogurt in the marinade tenderizes the meat and helps it soak up all the intense flavors of the *garam masala* (an Indian spice mixture). The nut crust, inspired by a recipe by Los Angeles chef Susan Feniger, seals in the meat juices and provides a rich, crunchy garnish.

> 1 4-pound boneless leg of lamb
> double recipe (2½ cups) Spiced Yogurt-Cilantro Sauce (page 157)
> 1 cup chopped pistachios
> 2 tablespoons brown sugar

The day before you plan to cook it, place the lamb in a large bowl and pour half of the yogurt-cilantro sauce over it, turning to coat completely. Reserve the remaining yogurt sauce to serve with the cooked lamb. Cover the lamb and the reserved yogurt mixture and refrigerate overnight.

Preheat oven to 400°F.

Remove lamb from marinade, scraping off and reserving most of the marinade, and place lamb, fat side up, in a roasting pan.

In a food processor or blender, combine the pistachios and brown sugar and process until nuts are coarsely ground. Add ¼ cup leftover marinade from the lamb (if you don't have ¼ cup, add some of the reserved yogurt-cilantro sauce) and process to combine. Spread this mixture evenly over the top of the lamb.

Roast lamb in preheated oven until it reaches 145°F on a meat thermometer, about 1 hour and 15 minutes (approximately 18 minutes per pound for medium-rare). Remove from oven and let stand 10 minutes. Slice the meat into ¼-inch-thick slices. Don't worry if the nut crust cracks off. Place a few slices of meat on each serving plate, drizzle with some of the reserved sauce, and garnish with a crumbling of the nut crust. Serve immediately.

Serve it with
+ Crunchy roasted potatoes
+ Steamed brown, white, or wild rice
+ Warm nan (Indian flatbread)

Steak au Poivre

The classic "steak with pepper" is standard issue at almost any traditional French restaurant. A perfect entrée to make for a date, it shows that you can cook *and* that you can afford expensive meat.

4 6-ounce beef tenderloins, about 1 inch thick
2 teaspoons kosher salt
2 tablespoons coarsely ground black pepper
2 tablespoons unsalted butter
2 tablespoons olive oil
½ cup Cognac
¾ cup heavy cream

Preheat oven to 350°F (optional).

Spread the salt and pepper evenly on a plate and press the steaks firmly into the mixture to form a peppery crust. Coat both sides well. Set aside.

Heat the butter and oil in a heavy skillet over medium-high heat until hot but not smoking, and cook steaks 4 to 6 minutes on each side. If you like your steaks medium-rare, transfer them to a platter while you whip up the sauce. Otherwise, transfer them to preheated oven until done to your preference.

Remove skillet from the heat and pour off any excess liquid, but don't wipe out the browned bits. Add Cognac carefully (there will be a big flare of steam and the Cognac will sizzle dramatically) and let boil over medium heat 1 minute. Add cream, stirring and scraping up the browned bits until sauce is reduced and thick enough to coat the back of a spoon (about 4 to 5 minutes). Pour sauce over steaks, and serve.

Serves 4.

Serve it with
+ Cauliflower and Goat Cheese Mash (page 139)
+ Roasted Asparagus with Lemon Vinaigrette (page 134)
+ Broccoli Rabe Sautéed with Garlic and Hot Pepper (page 135)

Change it up
+ Sauté a couple of minced shallots in the pan right after removing steaks and before adding Cognac and cream.
+ Add 2 teaspoons crushed fennel seeds with the salt and pepper.
+ Stir 1 teaspoon Dijon mustard into the sauce as it's cooking.

Chapter Nine

SIDES

Caramelized Fennel

One of the most powerful weapons in the Lazy Gourmet's arsenal is fennel. You probably didn't eat much fennel as a kid, but its versatility and unique flavor have made it a regular player on the menus of fine restaurants everywhere. Save the feathery fronds and chop them up as you would dill to add flavor to soups, pasta, or salads.

2 medium fennel bulbs, leafy tops trimmed and discarded (or saved for another use)
3 tablespoons olive oil
½ teaspoon kosher salt
1 tablespoon balsamic vinegar
1 ounce (about ⅓ cup) grated Parmesan cheese

Halve fennel bulbs, remove core, and thinly slice. Heat olive oil in a large skillet over medium heat. When oil is hot but not smoking, add fennel and cook, stirring occasionally, until soft and beginning to brown, about 30 minutes. Sprinkle with salt, stir in vinegar, and remove from heat. Serve topped with grated Parmesan.

Serves 2 to 4.

Serve it with
+ Five-Spice Roast Pork (page 126)
+ Steak au Poivre (page 129)

Butter-Braised Radishes

Radishes may be the forgotten stepchildren of the vegetable world, but these delightfully spicy little roots deserve royal treatment. Bathe them in butter with a touch of sugar and vinegar to bring out their regal qualities. We won't spoil the ending for you, but it's worth trying this dish just to watch the unexpected color transformation the radishes undergo.

2 tablespoons unsalted butter
1 small shallot, finely chopped
25–30 medium radishes, stems removed, halved or quartered
½ teaspoon sugar
½ teaspoon vinegar (white wine, champagne, red wine, sherry)
¼ teaspoon kosher salt
½ teaspoon freshly ground black pepper
½ cup water
1 tablespoon chopped fresh chives

In a large skillet, heat the butter over medium-high heat until butter is melted and starting to bubble. Reduce heat to medium, add shallot, and cook, stirring, until soft (about 2 minutes). Add the radishes, sugar, vinegar, salt, pepper, and water. Bring to a boil over medium-high heat, reduce heat to medium-low, cover, and simmer until the radishes are tender, about 6 to 8 minutes. Remove cover, return heat to medium-high, and cook, stirring, until most of the liquid has evaporated. Taste, and add additional salt and pepper if needed. Serve immediately, garnished with chives.

Serves 2 to 4.

Serve it with
+ Grilled sausages and sourdough baguette

Curried Sweet Peppers

Serve these colorful stunners as an appetizer with an assortment of fancy olives, cheeses, and crusty bread or as a side dish alongside meat or poultry. Leftovers make a tasty addition to sandwiches or salads.

> 4 bell peppers (any combination of red, yellow, orange)
> olive oil or olive oil spray
> 1 teaspoon curry powder
> ½ teaspoon kosher salt

Preheat broiler.

Remove the stems, seeds, and white membranes of the peppers and slice lengthwise into strips. Arrange the slices skin side down on a baking sheet and brush, drizzle, or spray with olive oil, coating thoroughly. Sprinkle the curry powder and salt over the peppers.

Broil for 8 to 10 minutes, until tender and a little charred around the edges.

Serves 4 to 6.

Make it ahead
The peppers can be stored, covered, in the fridge for a few days.

Serve it with
✦ Serve as part of an appetizer platter with crusty French bread, cured olives, and a selection of cheeses.
✦ Use leftovers in sandwiches and salads.

Roasted Asparagus with Lemon Vinaigrette

We love to serve this beautiful, elegant dish at brunches to add fresh color to a traditionally starch-and-egg-dominated meal—but it's also a perfect side for special lunches and dinners.

    2 pounds asparagus, woody ends snapped off
    olive oil or olive oil spray
    ½ teaspoon kosher salt
    2 tablespoons minced onion
    2 tablespoons Lemon Vinaigrette (page 148)

Preheat oven to 400°F.

Trim the ends off the asparagus spears to make them look nice and neat, and place them in a single layer on a baking sheet. Drizzle or spray with olive oil, turning to coat thoroughly. Sprinkle with salt. Roast in preheated oven for 15 to 20 minutes, depending on the thickness of the spears, until tender.

In a small bowl, combine the onion with the vinaigrette. Place asparagus on a serving platter and drizzle the vinaigrette mixture over them. Serve warm, at room temperature, or chilled.

Serves 4.

Make it ahead

The roasted asparagus can be refrigerated for up to 8 hours. Dress with the vinaigrette just before serving.

Change it up

✦ Top with crumbled feta or shaved Parmesan cheese.

Broccoli Rabe Sautéed with Garlic and Hot Pepper

This sublimely simple side uses the clever time- and dish-saving technique of steaming and sautéing vegetables in one step. Just drop your veggies in the skillet with both water *and* olive oil and they practically cook themselves. If you can't find broccoli rabe or baby broccoli, you can certainly substitute ordinary broccoli—but you have to admit, it won't seem quite as fancy.

¾ cup water
2 tablespoons olive oil
1 pound broccoli rabe or baby broccoli, trimmed, large stalks halved lengthwise
2–3 cloves garlic, minced
½ teaspoon kosher salt
¼–1 teaspoon crushed red pepper

Place water, olive oil, broccoli, garlic, salt, and crushed red pepper in a large skillet and cook over medium-high heat, covered, allowing the broccoli to steam. After 8 to 10 minutes, when the water has evaporated and the broccoli is fairly tender, remove the cover and stir to mix broccoli with the garlic, oil, and spices. Sauté the broccoli, stirring occasionally, 3 to 5 minutes more. Taste, and add additional salt and pepper if needed. Serve immediately.

Serves 2 to 4.

Serve it with
✦ Grilled or roasted meat or fish

Roasted Vegetables with Balsamic Syrup

A colorful platter of roasted vegetables is one of the easiest, healthiest, most delicious, and most visually striking dishes you can serve. Make a hearty sandwich with leftovers, like our Roasted Vegetable Sandwich with St. André Triple Cream Cheese (page 83) or a sandwich using our Spicy Feta Spread (page 45).

> **3 pounds of any combination of the following vegetables:**
> potatoes, small or cut into 1-inch-thick slices
> sweet potato, peeled and cut into 1-inch-thick slices
> cauliflower florets
> tomatoes, halved
> cherry tomatoes, whole
> onions, quartered
> radicchio, cut into 1-inch-thick slices
> winter squash (butternut, acorn, kabocha, etc.), peeled and cut into 1-inch-thick slices
> summer squash (zucchini, crookneck, etc.), cut into 1-inch-thick slices
> eggplant, cut into ½-inch-thick slices
> fennel bulbs, cut into ½-inch-thick slices
> mushrooms
> asparagus, woody ends snapped off
> olive oil or olive oil spray
> kosher salt to taste
> freshly ground black pepper to taste
> ½ cup Balsamic Syrup (page 147)

Preheat oven to 450°F.

Place vegetables on a baking sheet and drizzle, brush, or spray with olive oil, coating thoroughly. Sprinkle with a few pinches of salt and pepper. Bake in preheated oven until tender: soft vegetables like zucchini and mushrooms will cook faster (20 to 25 minutes) than firm vegetables like cauliflower and potatoes (40 to 50 minutes). Remove the quicker-roasting veggies as soon as they're done, and transfer them to a serving platter. When the slower-roasting veggies are done, add them to the platter.

Drizzle with balsamic syrup and serve.

Serves 4 to 6.

Serve it with

+ Roasted or grilled meats
+ Baked Polenta with Mascarpone and Corn (page 143)

Crispy Baked Rosemary Potatoes

This beyond-easy, unembellished dish never fails to please a crowd. It's like "comfort food plus." Serve alongside meat, poultry, or fish.

2 pounds small potatoes (such as red- or white-skinned new potatoes or Yukon Golds), halved
2 tablespoons olive oil
2 tablespoons chopped fresh rosemary
1 teaspoon kosher salt

Preheat oven to 400°F.

In a baking dish, toss potatoes with the oil, rosemary, and salt until thoroughly coated. Bake in preheated oven, stirring occasionally, about 1 hour, until potatoes are browned and crispy.

Serves 6.

Serve it with

+ Grilled, roasted, or braised meats
+ Duck Legs in Port Reduction (page 124)
+ Steak au Poivre (page 129)

Shredded Brussels Sprouts with Horseradish Cream

Even people who swear they hate Brussels sprouts love this dish. Well, actually we haven't tested that bold claim, but we strongly suspect it might be true. Invite some anti-Brussels friends over for dinner and conduct your own experiment!

> 2 tablespoons butter
> 2 tablespoons olive oil
> 1½ pounds Brussels sprouts, stem ends discarded, thinly sliced or shredded in a food processor
> ½ teaspoon kosher salt
> ½ teaspoon freshly ground pepper
> ¾ cup half-and-half
> 2 tablespoons prepared horseradish

In a large skillet, heat the butter and olive oil over medium-high heat until butter is melted and starting to bubble. Add sprouts, salt, and pepper. Cook, stirring occasionally, until sprouts are softened and lightly browned (3 to 7 minutes, depending on how thinly sliced they are). Stir in half-and-half and horseradish, lower heat to medium, and cook 3 to 7 minutes more, stirring occasionally, until sprouts are tender. Taste, and add additional salt, pepper, and horseradish if needed. Serve immediately.

Serves 4 to 6.

Serve it with
+ Grilled steak or roasted pork

Change it up
+ Leave out the half-and-half and horseradish, and halfway through cooking, stir in 2 minced cloves of garlic and the juice of two lemons.

Cauliflower and Goat Cheese Mash

Serve this dish instead of mashed potatoes to add a sophisticated touch to any meal. Diners who assume they're about to eat familiar fluffed spuds will be surprised and delighted by the subtle, unexpected flavor of this look-alike side.

1 head cauliflower (about 1½ pounds florets), cut into medium pieces
1 tablespoon unsalted butter
¼ cup whole milk
2 ounces chèvre
½ teaspoon kosher salt

Place the cauliflower in a vegetable steamer inside a large pot containing about an inch of water. Cover and bring to a boil over high heat. Reduce heat to low and simmer until cauliflower is tender, 10 to 15 minutes.

Put cauliflower, butter, milk, cheese, and salt in a food processor and process until smooth. (You can also blend it right in the cooking pot, after discarding the water, using an immersion blender.) Serve hot.

Serves 4 to 6.

Make it ahead

The mash can be stored, covered, in the fridge for a couple of days. Reheat gently in the microwave before serving.

Serve it with

✦ Roasted or grilled meats—as a fancy substitute for mashed potatoes
✦ Steak au Poivre (page 129)
✦ Five-Spice Roast Pork (page 126)

Change it up

✦ Add grated lemon zest or minced fresh herbs, such as basil or thyme.

Spiced Chard with Quinoa and Currants

Dress up your greens with a heady spice mixture, hearty quinoa, and sweet currants.

1 tablespoon olive oil
1 shallot, minced
1 bunch red chard, stems removed and leaves julienned
1 teaspoon ground cumin
1 teaspoon ground coriander
2 teaspoons paprika
½ teaspoon kosher salt
1 cup quinoa
⅓ cup currants
2 cups vegetable broth, chicken broth, or water

In a large skillet, heat the olive oil over medium heat. When oil is hot but not smoking, add the shallot and cook, stirring, about 3 minutes, until soft. Add chard, cumin, coriander, paprika, salt, quinoa, currants, and broth or water. Increase heat to medium-high and bring to a boil. Reduce heat to low, cover, and simmer 15 to 20 minutes, until all liquid has been absorbed and quinoa is light, fluffy, and expanded to about 3 times its original size. Taste, and add additional salt if needed.

Serves 2 to 4.

Serve it with
+ Chicken with Lemon and Olives (page 116)
+ Duck Legs in Port Reduction (page 124)

Change it up
+ Turn it into a quinoa gratin: spread the cooked quinoa mixture in an 8 x 8-inch baking dish, top with 1 cup of grated Gruyère, and bake at 500ºF for 10 minutes, or until cheese bubbles and begins to brown.
+ Stir in crumbled feta cheese just before serving.

Farro with Peas and Radishes

Farro is a hearty, protein-rich grain, known to have been domesticated in the Middle East as far back as 10,000 years ago. It makes an interesting alternative to rice—great with meat, fish, or as a bed for stews and stir-frys. There is some regional disagreement as to what exactly farro is—emmer, spelt, or einkorn. These cooking instructions are for emmer (*Triticum dicoccum*), so double-check your package and adjust your cooking method as indicated, if necessary. Farro can be found at international markets, health food stores, and many supermarkets.

1 cup farro
2½ cups chicken or vegetable broth
½ cup fresh or frozen peas
¼–½ teaspoon freshly ground black pepper
pinch of kosher salt
6 medium radishes, stemmed and thinly sliced

In a large saucepan with a tight-fitting lid, bring farro and broth to a boil over medium-high heat. Reduce heat to low and simmer, covered, until tender and chewy—30 to 45 minutes (15 to 20 minutes if using semi-pearled farro). Remove from heat, drain, and return to saucepan. Stir in peas and pepper. Taste, and add additional salt and pepper if needed. Serve garnished with radish slices.

Serves 4–6.

Make it ahead

Cooked farro will keep, covered, in the fridge for a few days. Add radish slices just before serving.

Serve it with

✦ Duck Legs in Port Reduction (page 124)
✦ Spicy Chicken Mole (page 120)
✦ Grilled or roasted meats, stews, or stir-frys

Change it up

✦ Top with crumbled feta or a grated hard cheese like Parmesan or Asiago.

Quinoa Pilaf with Brussels Sprouts and Carrots

The ancient Incas referred to quinoa (pronounced keen-wah) as "the mother of all grains" for good reason. Turns out it still merits the superlative title: it's both extremely tasty and really, really good for you. Once sidelined as "hippie food," these days you can find quinoa on the hippest tables in town.

3 tablespoons olive oil
1 large onion, diced
¾ pound Brussels sprouts, stemmed and quartered lengthwise
1 large carrot, peeled and diced
1 cup quinoa
2 cups chicken or vegetable broth or water
1 teaspoon kosher salt
¼–½ teaspoon freshly ground black pepper
½ cup toasted pine nuts

In a large skillet or stock pot, heat oil over medium-high heat until hot but not smoking. Add onions and Brussels sprouts, reduce heat to medium, and cook, stirring occasionally, for 8 to 10 minutes, until onions are browned but not burnt and Brussels sprouts are browned and beginning to soften. Add carrots, quinoa, broth or water, salt, and pepper and stir, scraping up browned bits from the bottom of the pan. Bring to a boil, reduce heat to low, cover, and simmer until all liquid is absorbed and quinoa is light, fluffy, and expanded to about 3 times its original size, about 15 to 20 minutes. Stir in pine nuts, and serve.

Serves 6 to 8.

Serve it with
+ Chicken with Lemon and Olives (page 116)
+ Roasted Salmon with Garlic Confit (page 107)

Change it up
+ Stir in crumbled feta cheese just before serving.
+ Toss in chopped fresh herbs like thyme, oregano, basil, or rosemary.

Baked Polenta with Mascarpone and Corn

Polenta may be nothing more than a humble cornmeal gruel, but those ancient Romans were on to something. It is a versatile, delicious companion to all kinds of entrées—and this baked version, rich with cheese, does away with the drudgery of standing over the stovetop and stirring, making a classic favorite *even* easier to prepare.

    1 cup dry polenta
    3½ cups water
    1 cup sweet corn kernels, fresh (from about 1 ear) or frozen
    1 teaspoon kosher salt
    ½ teaspoon freshly ground black pepper
    1 ounce (about ⅓ cup) grated Parmesan cheese
    ¼ cup mascarpone
    2 tablespoons butter

Preheat oven to 350°F. Oil an 8 x 8-inch baking dish.

In baking dish, combine polenta, water, corn, salt, and pepper, stirring to mix. Bake in preheated oven, uncovered, for 50 minutes. Stir in Parmesan, mascarpone, and butter, return to the oven, and bake another 10 minutes. Spoon onto plates or into bowls, and serve topped with your favorite sauce, or as a side dish.

Serves 4 to 6.

Serve it with

+ Roasted Vegetables with Balsamic Syrup (page 136)
+ Duck Legs in Port Reduction (page 124)
+ Sautéed mushrooms or your favorite tomato-based pasta sauce

Change it up

+ Stir in minced fresh rosemary, basil, or oregano after baking.
+ Cool to room temperature and refrigerate, covered, for a few hours or overnight. Slide the chilled polenta out of the dish and cut it into squares or triangles. Heat polenta slices in the oven or cook them in butter or olive oil in a large, heavy skillet over medium-high heat until browned, about 2 minutes per side. Serve hot, topped with sauce or cheese, or alongside roasted meats.

Cumin-Raisin Couscous

Couscous may look like a grain, but it's actually a tiny little pasta made by rolling and shaping semolina wheat. This versatile Mediterranean staple is known to have existed as far back as the 13th century, and makes for an interesting alternative to rice or pasta.

1½ cups couscous
1½ cups boiling water
3 tablespoons unsalted butter, cut into pieces
¾ cup raisins
¾ cup toasted slivered almonds
1 tablespoon ground cumin
½ teaspoon kosher salt
¼–½ teaspoon freshly ground black pepper

In a medium serving bowl, mix couscous, boiling water, and butter and stir with a fork to combine. Cover and let sit for 5 to 10 minutes, and then fluff with a fork. Mix in raisins, almonds, cumin, salt, and pepper. Taste, and add additional salt and pepper if needed.

Serves 4 to 6.

Make it ahead

The couscous can be kept in the fridge, covered, for a couple of days. Serve at room temperature or reheat a minute or two in the microwave.

Serve it with

✦ Moroccan-Spiced Cornish Game Hens with Lemon and Mint (page 122)
✦ Top Sirloin with Charmoula on a Bed of Arugula (page 113)
✦ Roasted Salmon with Garlic Confit (page 107)

Change it up

✦ For a striking presentation, try using extra-large Israeli couscous in place of regular couscous, cooking according to the instructions on the package.

Coconut Rice

Plain steamed rice is nice enough, but this rich, flavorful version is much, much nicer.

vegetable oil or vegetable oil spray
2 cups basmati rice
2 cups (1 15-ounce can) coconut milk
water
pinch of kosher salt

Coat the bottom of a large saucepan (one with a tight-fitting lid) with vegetable oil or vegetable oil spray. Cook rice according to the instructions on the package, adding a pinch of salt and replacing half of the water with coconut milk. (You probably won't need to use the full 2 cups of coconut milk.) When rice is cooked, fluff with a fork, and serve hot.

Serves 6 to 8.

Make it ahead

Coconut rice can be kept, covered, in the refrigerator for a couple of days. To serve, place in a microwave-safe bowl, sprinkle with a bit of water, cover with plastic wrap, and heat briefly in the microwave.

Serve it with

✦ Five-Spice Roast Pork (page 126) or any spicy Asian stir-fry dish

Change it up

✦ For added texture and coconut flavor, add ¼ to ½ cup of unsweetened shredded coconut with the rice, or garnish with toasted unsweetened shredded coconut.
✦ If you have a rice cooker, simply add all of the ingredients to the rice cooker, turn it on, and cook as you would cook plain rice.

Rice, Barley, Lentil, and Mushroom Pilaf

This hearty, flavorful combo is a perfect substitute for plain rice—and almost as easy to make.

½ cup brown rice
½ cup pearl barley
½ cup dried lentils
3⅓ cups chicken or vegetable broth
2 teaspoons Dijon mustard
1 tablespoon soy sauce
1 ounce dried mushrooms, any type, rinsed and chopped

In a large saucepan, combine rice, barley, lentils, broth, mustard, soy sauce, and mushrooms. Stir briskly to break up the mustard. Bring to a boil over high heat. Reduce heat to low and simmer, covered, 45 to 55 minutes, or until all liquid is absorbed.

Serves 4 to 6.

Serve it with
✦ Steak au Poivre (page 129)
✦ Pomegranate-Roasted Chicken with Figs and Ginger (page 117)

Chapter Ten

CONDIMENTS, SAUCES, AND EXTRAS

Balsamic Syrup

This sweet and tangy syrup is perfect drizzled over grilled vegetables (page 136), grilled chicken or fish, fine cheeses, fruit, and even ice cream. (See Pistachio Ice Cream with Strawberries and Balsamic Syrup, page 176.)

1½ cups balsamic vinegar

In a wide saucepan or skillet, bring vinegar to a boil over medium-high heat. Reduce heat to medium-low and simmer until it is reduced to about one-third its original quantity and is thick and syrupy enough to coat the back of a spoon, 15 to 20 minutes.

Makes ½ cup.

Make it ahead

The syrup can be stored, covered, in the fridge for a really, really long time. Bring to room temperature or reheat over medium heat before serving.

Lemon Vinaigrette

This magical dressing can be used on just about any vegetable or salad. Try it on our Roasted Asparagus (page 134) or Warm Jerusalem Artichoke Salad (page 67). Drizzle it over Brussels sprouts, broccoli, or zucchini, or any other cooked vegetables. It's so versatile that you can even use it as a marinade for chicken or fish.

3 tablespoons lemon juice (from about 1 lemon)
1 tablespoon champagne vinegar or white wine vinegar
1 small clove garlic, minced
1 to 2 teaspoons sugar, depending on the sweetness of your lemons
½ teaspoon kosher salt
¼–½ teaspoon freshly ground black pepper
¼ cup olive oil

In a small bowl or a jar with a tight-fitting lid, combine lemon juice, vinegar, garlic, sugar, salt, and pepper. Add olive oil and whisk or shake vigorously until well combined. Taste, and add additional salt and pepper if needed.

Makes about ½ cup.

Make it ahead
The vinaigrette can be stored in the fridge for a couple of days. If the oil solidifies, set the vinaigrette on the counter and allow it to come to room temperature and liquefy again before dressing your salad.

Serve it with
✦ Roasted Asparagus (page 134)
✦ Artichoke and Endive Panzanella (page 63)
✦ Warm Jerusalem Artichoke Salad (page 67)
✦ Any mixed salad or cooked vegetable
✦ Artichoke hearts, or as a dip for artichoke leaves

Change it up
✦ Mix in minced shallot or onion.
✦ Add any fresh or dried herbs you like, such as basil or oregano.

Balsamic Vinaigrette

Why buy dressing in a bottle when it's *this* easy to make? Sweet balsamic vinegar is a perfect complement to a salad made with bitter greens like arugula and radicchio (see Salad of Bitter Greens with Asiago, page 60).

3 tablespoons balsamic vinegar
½ teaspoon Dijon mustard
½ teaspoon kosher salt
¼–½ teaspoon freshly ground black pepper
¼ cup olive oil

In a small bowl or a jar with a tight-fitting lid, combine vinegar, mustard, salt, and pepper. Add olive oil and whisk or shake vigorously until well combined. Taste, and add additional salt and pepper if needed.

Makes about ½ cup.

Make it ahead
The vinaigrette can be stored in the fridge for a couple of days. If the oil solidifies, set the vinaigrette on the counter and allow it to come to room temperature and liquefy again before dressing your salad.

Serve it with
✦ Salad of Bitter Greens with Asiago (page 60) or any mixed green salad

Change it up
✦ Add 1 clove minced garlic.
✦ Add a tablespoon of any fresh chopped herbs (rosemary, oregano, thyme, etc.).

Sherry-Shallot Vinaigrette

A good-quality sherry vinegar and minced shallots give this dressing powerful flavor.

2 tablespoons sherry vinegar
½ teaspoon Dijon mustard
1 tablespoon minced shallots
½ teaspoon sugar
½ teaspoon kosher salt
¼–½ teaspoon freshly ground black pepper
¼ cup olive oil

In a small bowl or a jar with a tightly fitting lid, combine vinegar, mustard, shallots, sugar, salt, and pepper. Add olive oil and whisk or shake vigorously until well combined. Taste, and add additional salt and pepper if needed.

Makes about ½ cup.

Make it ahead

The vinaigrette can be stored in the fridge for a couple of days. If the oil solidifies, set the vinaigrette on the counter and allow it to come to room temperature and liquefy again before dressing your salad.

Serve it with

✦ Pear, Escarole, and Blue Cheese Salad (page 58) or any mixed green salad

Wasabi-Lime Vinaigrette

The Japanese wasabi radish gives this refreshing dressing a surprising kick. You can find wasabi paste or powder (just mix with equal parts water to make it into a paste) in the Asian foods aisle of many supermarkets or in Asian specialty markets.

3 tablespoons lime juice (from about 2 limes)
2 teaspoons honey
1 tablespoon soy sauce
1–3 teaspoons wasabi paste, or to taste
¼ cup vegetable oil

In a small bowl or a jar with a tight-fitting lid, combine lime juice, honey, soy sauce, and 1 teaspoon wasabi paste and whisk or shake until the honey and wasabi dissolve. Add oil and whisk or shake vigorously until well combined. Taste, and add more wasabi paste as desired, whisking or shaking until wasabi is dissolved and well combined.

Makes about ¾ cup.

Make it ahead

The vinaigrette can be stored in the fridge, covered, for a couple of days. If the oil solidifies, set the vinaigrette on the counter and allow it to come to room temperature and liquefy again before dressing your salad.

Serve it with

✦ Chilled Soba Noodle Salad with Shrimp, Avocado, and Grapefruit (page 68)
✦ A salad of lettuce, thinly sliced radish, and cucumber

Change it up

✦ Mix in minced pickled ginger or garnish your salad with toasted sesame seeds.

Compound Butters

Elevate your meals to a whole new level with one of our simplest and most delicious Lazy Gourmet tips. Compound butters (*beurre composé* in French) are simply softened butter with other ingredients mixed in. They're incredibly easy to make, allow limitless creativity, taste heavenly, and can be made well ahead. Enjoy them tossed with hot pasta to make an instant sauce, or on baked potatoes, sweet potatoes, warm bread, scones, pancakes, fish, meat, vegetables, corn on the cob—absolutely anything you'd put ordinary butter on.

To make any of the following compound butters, just soften one stick (½ cup) of unsalted butter and add the ingredients listed. After mixing thoroughly, transfer the compound butter to a lovely little serving dish, cover, and chill. Let soften a little before serving.

These recipes make enough for several uses, so feel free to halve them. Or, even better, make the full amount and place any extra on a square of plastic wrap, form it into a log, and freeze for up to several months. Slice off a round whenever you need a little something to fancy up a piece of grilled meat, fish, or bread.

GARLIC-HERB BUTTER

1 teaspoon kosher salt
¼–½ teaspoon freshly ground black pepper
½–1 teaspoon crushed red pepper
4 cloves garlic, minced
1 tablespoon minced fresh rosemary
1 tablespoon red wine (optional)

MOROCCAN SPICED BUTTER WITH LEMON AND MINT

3 cloves garlic, minced
grated zest of 2 lemons
6 tablespoons lemon juice (from about 2 lemons)
¼ cup minced fresh mint
1 teaspoon paprika
1 teaspoon ground cumin
½ teaspoon kosher salt
¼–½ teaspoon freshly ground black pepper

GORGONZOLA BUTTER

5 ounces (about 1 cup) crumbled Gorgonzola
    cheese
1 medium shallot, minced

CHIPOTLE-HONEY BUTTER

¼ cup honey
¼ cup minced cilantro
2 tablespoons seeded and minced chipotle chiles
    from a can of *chipotles en adobo*
1 tablespoon lime juice (from about half a lime)
1 teaspoon kosher salt

SUN-DRIED TOMATO BUTTER

2 rounded tablespoons minced sundried tomato
    (packed in oil)
1 clove garlic, minced
1 teaspoon kosher salt

LEMON, CAPER, AND CHIVE BUTTER

1 heaping tablespoon minced chives
1 tablespoon small capers, drained and minced
grated zest of 1 lemon
3 tablespoons lemon juice (from about 1 lemon)
½ teaspoon kosher salt

SIMON AND GARFUNKEL BUTTER

2 teaspoons minced fresh flat leaf parsley
2 teaspoons minced fresh sage
2 teaspoons minced fresh rosemary
2 teaspoons minced fresh thyme
1 teaspoon kosher salt

LAVENDER-HONEY BUTTER

1 teaspoon culinary lavender*
¼ cup honey
½ teaspoon kosher salt

* Buy dried culinary lavender, grown specifically for cooking, in the spice section of your supermarket, from a specialty gourmet shop, or online.

TRUFFLE BUTTER

1 tablespoon truffle oil
½ teaspoon kosher salt

HONEY-PECAN BUTTER

⅓ cup chopped toasted pecans
¼ cup honey

Make it ahead

Compound butters can be stored in the fridge for a couple of weeks (a couple of days if the butter uses raw garlic), or in the freezer for several months. For freezer storage, roll the butter into a log shape using a sheet of plastic wrap. Place the wrapped butter log in a ziplock bag clearly marked with the type of butter it contains and the date it was made.

Lemon-Raisin Salsa

This sweet, tart, colorful salsa is stunningly delicious served as an appetizer with crusty bread and goat cheese, or it can be used to transform simple baked, grilled, or roasted fish or chicken into something really special.

> 2 whole medium lemons
> ½ cup minced raisins
> 2 tablespoons minced onion
> 1 tablespoon olive oil
> 2 teaspoons sugar
> ½ teaspoon kosher salt
> ¼ cup (loosely packed) minced cilantro

Slice off and discard all the lemon rind and bitter pith. Chop the remaining lemon flesh into small pieces. Remove seeds and discard any thick pieces of membrane. Scrape the chopped lemon and any juice that has collected on your cutting board into a small bowl. Mix in raisins, onion, olive oil, sugar, salt, and cilantro.

Makes 1 cup of salsa.

Make it ahead

> While it will stay delicious stored, covered, in the fridge for a couple of days, this salsa looks most vibrant and colorful within the first couple of hours after preparation. If you want to make it ahead and have it look great, add the cilantro just before serving.

Serve it with

> ✦ Baked or pan-fried fish, like Baked Tilapia with Lemon-Raisin Salsa (page 91)
> ✦ Seared sea scallops
> ✦ Grilled or roasted chicken
> ✦ Smoked salmon or lox
> ✦ Prosciutto and Taleggio Sandwich with Lemon-Raisin Salsa (page 88)

Change it up

> ✦ Replace the cilantro with basil or parsley.

Charmoula

This zesty, spicy North African condiment—a great partner for fish, chicken, steak, lamb, or bean dishes—improves in flavor as it sits and the flavors meld. Don't stress about painstakingly plucking each and every cilantro leaf off the stem; you can toss the thin stems right in (not the larger, woodier ones).

6 medium cloves garlic, peeled
1 large jalapeño chile, stemmed, seeded, and finely minced
½ cup (tightly packed) fresh cilantro (leaves and thin stems)
½ cup (tightly packed) fresh mint
1 tablespoon paprika
1 tablespoon ground cumin
1 teaspoon kosher salt
¼ cup lemon juice (from about 1½ lemons)
3 tablespoons olive oil

Mince the garlic, chile, cilantro, and mint by hand or in a food processor and place in a medium bowl. Stir in paprika, cumin, and salt. Add lemon juice and olive oil and stir to mix well. Let sit at least 30 minutes before using.

Makes about ⅔ cup.

Make it ahead
    Charmoula can be stored, covered, in the fridge for a couple of days.

Serve it with
    ✦ Top Sirloin with Charmoula on a Bed of Arugula (page 113)
    ✦ Lamb Burgers with Feta Cheese and Charmoula (page 123)
    ✦ Moroccan Chickpea Stew with Charmoula (page 108)
    ✦ Pasta with summer vegetables and feta cheese

Lemon-Tahini Dip

This tangy dip calls for tahini, a paste made from ground sesame seeds. A staple of Mediterranean cooking, tahini can be found at international markets, in health food stores, and many grocery stores. We love this dip with artichokes (page 48) but it's also perfect for crudités or pita chips, as a sandwich spread, or thinned out with a little extra lemon juice and used as a salad dressing.

½ cup plain, whole-milk yogurt
¾ cup lemon juice (from about 2 lemons)
2 tablespoons tahini
2 teaspoons sugar
1 teaspoon kosher salt
¼–½ teaspoon freshly ground black pepper

In a medium bowl, combine the yogurt, lemon juice, tahini, sugar, salt, and pepper and mix until well combined.

Makes about 1 cup.

Make it ahead

The dip can be kept in the fridge, covered, for a couple of days.

Serve it with
+ Steamed artichokes (page 48)
+ A chopped salad of romaine lettuce, halved cherry tomatoes, cucumber, and sliced Kalamata olives
+ Fresh endive, red and yellow bell peppers, blanched green beans, and other crudités for dipping
+ Crunchy pita chips for dipping
+ Baked, broiled, or grilled salmon or other fish

Change it up
+ Thin with additional lemon juice or water and use as a dressing.

Spiced Yogurt-Cilantro Sauce

It would be nearly impossible for us to choose our favorite condiment, but if we had to, this tart, tangy, flavorful sauce would be a top contender. We use it as a spread for our Bombay-Style Vegetable Sandwiches (page 85) and as a marinade for our Pistachio-Crusted Roast Leg of Lamb (page 128).

1 medium clove garlic, peeled
1 2-inch piece fresh ginger, peeled and cut into chunks
1–3 small Serrano chiles, stemmed and seeded
1 cup (tightly packed) fresh cilantro (leaves and thin stems)
1 cup plain whole-milk yogurt
2 tablespoons garam masala*
grated zest of 1 lime
3 tablespoons lime juice (from about 2 limes)
1 teaspoon kosher salt

* If you can't find garam masala, you can substitute individual spices: 1½ teaspoons each ground cumin, coriander, and cardamom; 1 teaspoon ground black pepper; ½ teaspoon ground cinnamon; and ¼ teaspoon each ground cloves and nutmeg.

In a food processor or by hand, mince the garlic, ginger, chiles, and cilantro and place in a medium bowl. Stir in yogurt, garam masala, lime zest, lime juice, and salt and until well combined.

Makes about 1¼ cups.

Make it ahead

The sauce can be made a couple of days ahead and stored, covered, in the fridge.

Serve it with

✦ Pistachio-Crusted Roast Leg of Lamb (page 128)
✦ Bombay-Style Vegetable Sandwiches (page 85)
✦ Roasted or grilled vegetables, such as eggplant, zucchini, cauliflower, or potatoes

Change it up

✦ Use fresh mint in place of the cilantro.
✦ Add ½ cup roasted peanuts with the garlic, ginger, and chiles.
✦ Add ½ cup unsweetened shredded coconut.

Fig and Onion Jam

You might be wondering why a Lazy Gourmet would want to make jam from scratch when it's so easy to buy jam in a jar. First, this is no ordinary store jam. Second, it's *really* easy to make. This sweet-savory delicacy is a stunning addition to an antipasto plate and pairs well with salty, sharp cheeses like Gorgonzola, Manchego, or Parmesan or milder, tangier cheeses like chèvre. Try it alongside roasted or grilled meats like pork, chicken, or spicy sausages.

2 tablespoons olive oil
1 small onion, diced
15 medium fresh black mission figs, stemmed and diced
1 cup red wine
½ cup water
¾ cup sugar
¼ teaspoon kosher salt

Heat oil in a wide, shallow saucepan or skillet over medium-high heat. When oil is hot but not smoking, add onions and sauté until soft and translucent, 5 to 7 minutes. Add figs and cook a few minutes more, until the fruit begins to soften. Add wine, water, sugar, and salt and bring to a boil. Lower heat to medium-low and simmer 40 to 60 minutes (time will vary depending on the width of your pan), stirring occasionally, until mixture is thick and syrupy. Stir a little more frequently toward the end, to prevent burning. Serve warm or at room temperature.

Makes about 1½ cups.

Make it ahead

The jam can be made ahead and stored, covered, in the refrigerator for a couple of weeks. Enjoy it cold, or warm it up briefly in the microwave before serving.

Serve it with

+ Cheeses like Gorgonzola, Manchego, Parmesan, or chèvre
+ An antipasto platter
+ Meats like roast pork or chicken
+ Savory Blue Cheese Shortbread (page 38)

Change it up

+ When fresh figs aren't available, you can substitute dried figs. Soak 6 ounces (about 1 cup) dried figs in hot water for 30 minutes to rehydrate, and follow the rest of the directions as written.

Plum and Currant Mostarda

This tangy and pungent Italian condiment, similar to chutney, is ideal for dressing up a cheese platter, charcuterie plate, or simple roast pork. The intense dark-red color really brightens up the room.

⅔ cup sugar
¾ cup white wine
1 cup currants
10 medium plums (about 2 pounds), pitted and diced
¼ cup Dijon mustard
¼ cup white wine vinegar
2 tablespoons whole mustard seeds

Combine the sugar and wine in a nonreactive saucepan (page 25) and bring to a boil over medium-high heat. Add the currants and reduce heat to low. Simmer very gently about 10 minutes, until currants are soft. Add the plums, mustard, wine vinegar, and mustard seeds. Increase heat to medium-high and bring back to a boil. Reduce heat to low again and continue to simmer 20 to 40 minutes more (time will vary depending on the width of your pan), until mixture thickens to a jam-like consistency.

Makes about 2 cups.

Make it ahead

Mostarda can be kept, covered in the fridge, for up to a week.

Serve it with

✦ Strong, salty cheeses, such as Gorgonzola, Parmesan, or Manchego and cured meats like prosciutto or salami
✦ Roasted or grilled meats, including pork, chicken, or fish
✦ Savory Blue Cheese Shortbread (page 38)

Change it up

✦ Replace the plums and currants with any fresh and dried fruit combination. Try fresh peaches and dried cherries, fresh rhubarb and golden raisins, or fresh pears and dried apricots.

Crispy Fried Sage Leaves

These crisp, fragrant leaves make a delicious garnish for many pasta and vegetable dishes. Using a saucepan instead of a skillet helps to minimize the splattering, but you still might want to wear an apron and take care to protect yourself and your clothes from the hot oil.

> vegetable oil
> 1 or 2 bunches of fresh sage leaves, stems removed
> kosher salt

Pour about ½ inch of vegetable oil into a saucepan and heat over high heat. When the oil starts to shimmer, toss in a small sage leaf to test the heat—if it sizzles and crackles, your oil is hot enough for frying. Fry the sage leaves in several small batches about 10 to 20 seconds per batch. Keep a good eye on them, pulling them out of the oil when they've shriveled, darkened a little in color, and feel stiff when tapped with a spoon—but before they turn brown. Later batches, as the oil gets even hotter, will fry quicker than earlier batches, so adjust your timing as needed. Using a slotted spoon, transfer the leaves to a paper towel and let them drain and cool. Season to taste with salt.

Make it ahead

The sage leaves can be prepared 1 to 2 days ahead and stored in an airtight container at room temperature.

Serve it with

+ Pasta with Butternut Squash (page 106)
+ Savory Pumpkin and Sage Flan (page 95)
+ Butternut squash or pumpkin soup

Parmesan Lace

This crispy, cheesy garnish is great on salads and in soups. In fact it's so good you might want to make extra and have it as a snack with sliced apples—or even just by itself.

4 ounces (about 1⅓ cups) grated Parmesan cheese

Preheat oven to 350°F. Lightly oil a baking sheet.

Scatter the grated cheese on the baking sheet in a loose layer about ⅛ to ¼ inch thick. (You don't want the layer to be too thin, or the cheese won't hold together.) Alternatively, you can drop the cheese into small, separate circles instead of one big sheet. Bake the cheese in the preheated oven 3 to 6 minutes, until cheese is lightly browned and bubbly; check it every couple of minutes to make sure it doesn't burn. Remove the cheese from the oven and allow to cool for a couple of minutes. Scrape the crispy baked cheese off the baking sheet with a metal spatula. If it's in one big sheet, break it up into a few smaller pieces.

Make it ahead

The Parmesan lace can be stored, covered, in the fridge for a couple of days. Bring to room temperature before serving.

Serve it with

✦ Caramelized Onion Soup (page 69)
✦ Any soup that would be good with cheese
✦ Any salad that would be good with cheese

Roasted Garlic

While raw garlic is too strong for most people to chomp down like a snack food, roasted garlic is thoroughly edible, with a sweeter, mellower flavor and smooth, spreadable texture. This simple appetizer looks beautiful, makes a great conversation piece, and tastes amazing on bread or crackers. Use leftovers in stews, soups, or pastas; or on meat, fish, vegetables, or baked potatoes.

1 or more heads (bulbs) of garlic
olive oil

Preheat oven to 400°F.

Peel away and discard the loose, papery outer layers of skin. Slice the top ½ inch off the pointed end of the bulb, exposing a nice cross section of the cloves inside. Place each bulb, cut side up, on a square of aluminum foil large enough to wrap the bulb in. Drizzle a tablespoon or so of olive oil over the cut side of each garlic bulb, and wrap tightly in the foil. Bake 45 to 60 minutes, until cloves are browned and very soft.

Let guests squeeze the soft cloves out of their skins with a small butter knife or cocktail fork. Spread on bread or crackers.

Make it ahead
Roasted garlic can be stored, covered, in the fridge for several days.

Serve it with
+ Warm bread, a dish of olive oil, and assorted cured olives
+ Roasted Salmon with Garlic Confit (page 107)
+ Grilled chicken, steak, or seafood

Homemade Croutons

Making your own croutons from scratch could not be easier, and they are so much more impressive and better tasting than the store-bought variety. Use any crusty bread you have lying around—it can even be stale. Try a specialty bread made with herbs, nuts, or dried fruits, to add even more personality to your soups and salads.

4 cups cubed bread
¼ cup olive oil
½ teaspoon kosher salt
½–1 teaspoon freshly ground black pepper

Preheat oven to 300°F.

Place bread cubes in a single layer in a baking dish. Drizzle olive oil over cubes in a slow, steady stream, tossing vigorously to coat all pieces equally. Sprinkle with salt and pepper. Bake 30 to 40 minutes, turning once, until croutons are crisp and golden brown. Let cool a little before tossing into salads, but go ahead and toss into soups while they're still nice and hot.

Make it ahead

Croutons will keep in an airtight container on the countertop for a few days. If you make a cheesy version (see below), store them in the fridge and bring them to room temperature before serving. For long-term preservation, store them in the freezer. Just leave them out on the countertop to thaw and return to room temperature, and they'll be as good as new.

Serve it with

✦ Just about any soup or salad

Change it up

✦ Mix 2 cloves minced garlic into olive oil mixture.

✦ Mix herbs and spices in with the olive oil: ground coriander, rosemary, basil, oregano, fennel, thyme, marjoram—or just about anything you find in your spice rack.

✦ Sprinkle croutons with ⅓ cup grated Parmesan cheese 5 minutes before the end of baking.

✦ For a blue cheese variation, leave out the salt and pepper. After baking about 25 minutes, remove baking dish from oven and sprinkle cheese over the bread cubes. Return dish to oven and bake 5 minutes, until cheese is melted. Toss bread cubes to coat with the cheese, spread out again in a single layer, and bake another 10 to 15 minutes, until croutons are crisp and golden brown.

Raspberry Coulis

This jewel-toned sauce takes just seconds to prepare and can beautify even the plainest cake or dish of ice cream.

¾ cup frozen unsweetened raspberries, defrosted
2 tablespoons sugar

Purée raspberries and sugar in a food processor until smooth. If needed, add water, a tablespoon at a time, until it reaches the consistency of a light syrup. Strain liquid through a fine-meshed sieve to remove solids.

Makes about ½ cup.

Make it ahead
> The coulis can be stored, covered, in the fridge for about a week.

Serve it with
- ✦ Crème Fraîche and Buttermilk Ice Cream (page 174), or store-bought vanilla or chocolate ice cream
- ✦ Miniature Flourless Chocolate Cakes (page 183)
- ✦ Chocolate Indulgence (page 181)
- ✦ Chocolate Ricotta Turnovers (page 182)

Change it up
- ✦ Substitute blackberries for the raspberries.

Bittersweet Chocolate Drizzle

This rich chocolate concoction takes less than 5 minutes to prepare. Drizzle it over ice cream (try it on our Crème Fraîche and Buttermilk Ice Cream, page 174, Pink Peppercorn Ice Cream, page 173, or even just regular store-bought vanilla), over cake (it's the perfect partner for our Orange Crème Fraîche Cake, page 184), or Poached Pears (page 177).

½ to ⅔ cup heavy cream
4 ounces bittersweet or semisweet baking chocolate, chopped
2 tablespoons unsalted butter, diced
pinch of salt

Place ½ cup cream, chocolate, butter, and salt in a microwave-safe dish and heat on high for 1 minute, or until cream begins to boil. Stir to melt butter and chocolate. If you want a thinner sauce, simply add a touch more cream.

Makes about 1 cup.

Make it ahead
  The sauce can be stored, covered, in the fridge for a couple of days. Reheat gently in the microwave before serving.

Serve it with
  ✦ Ice cream
  ✦ Fresh fruit
  ✦ Fruit-filled crepes
  ✦ Orange Crème Fraîche Cake (page 184)
  ✦ Poached Pears (page 177)

Change it up
  ✦ When chocolate is fully melted, stir in the finely grated zest of a small orange or a couple of tablespoons of orange- or coffee-flavored liqueur.

Chapter Eleven

DESSERTS

Sweet Peach Crostini

While crostini are usually served as appetizers, topped with various savory delights, this sweet version makes a perfect light dessert or midday snack.

1 10-ounce skinny baguette
12 ounces (about 1½ cups) mascarpone cheese
¾ cup peach preserves
½ cup toasted shelled pistachios

Preheat oven to 400°F.

Slice baguette about ½ inch thick and place on a baking sheet. Bake in preheated oven for 5 to 7 minutes, or until lightly toasted and crunchy. Spread about half a tablespoon mascarpone on each slice, followed by a dollop of peach preserves and a sprinkle of pistachios.

Makes about 40 crostini.

Change it up
- ✦ Experiment with other flavors of preserves, such as blackberry or plum.
- ✦ Instead of preserves, use fresh berries or sliced peaches and a drizzle of honey.
- ✦ Instead of pistachios, try pine nuts, chopped pecans, or sliced almonds.
- ✦ Substitute cream cheese, crème fraîche, ricotta, Brie, or even Cambozola for the mascarpone.

Lemon-Lavender Butter Cookies

These simple, delicate cookies pack a surprising hint of flowery lavender flavor. Be sure to buy lavender intended for cooking, which you can find in the spice section of your supermarket or in specialty shops.

> 1 cup sugar
> grated zest of 1 lemon
> 2 teaspoons lavender
> 1 cup (2 sticks) unsalted butter, softened
> 1 large egg
> 3 tablespoons lemon juice (from about 1 lemon)
> 1 tablespoon vanilla extract
> 1 teaspoon baking powder
> pinch of table salt
> 2½ cups all-purpose flour
> decorating sugar (optional)

Place sugar and lemon zest in a large mixing bowl. Add lavender, rubbing between the palms of your hands to crush the buds a bit. Rub sugar, lemon zest, and lavender together until well incorporated and the sugar becomes damp. Add butter and beat with an electric mixer or by hand, until fluffy. Add egg and mix until incorporated. Add lemon juice and vanilla and mix well. Add baking powder, salt, and 1 cup of flour. Beat until mixed well. Add another cup of flour and continue to beat until mixed well. Add remaining ½ cup of flour and beat until incorporated. Divide dough in half, wrap each half in plastic wrap, and form it into a log about 8 inches long and 2 inches in diameter. Refrigerate at least 1 hour and as long as three days.

Preheat oven to 400°F.

Remove dough from refrigerator and slice into thin rounds using a very sharp or serrated knife. (Alternatively, dough can be rolled out on a lightly floured board and cut with cookie cutters.) Place cookies about 1 inch apart on a large ungreased baking sheet. Sprinkle with decorating sugar if desired and bake in preheated oven for 10 to 15 minutes, until edges just begin to brown. Allow to cool on baking sheet for a minute or two, and then quickly remove to a wire rack to cool completely. (If you let them sit too long, they'll stick and be impossible to remove in one piece.)

Makes 50 to 60 cookies.

Make it ahead

Uncooked dough can be stored, tightly wrapped, in the fridge for several days, or in the freezer for up to a month. To freeze, wrap each log tightly in plastic wrap and store in a heavy-duty freezer storage bag. When ready to bake cookies, use a very sharp knife to slice frozen dough into thin rounds and bake as directed above. Baked cookies will keep, stored at room temperature in an airtight container, for several days.

Serve it with

✦ Crème Fraîche and Buttermilk Ice Cream (page 174) or store-bought strawberry or vanilla ice cream

Change it up

✦ Leave out the lavender for simple but lovely lemon butter cookies.

✦ Substitute 2 tablespoons fresh mint or basil for the lavender.

✦ Substitute orange zest and orange juice for the lemon zest and juice.

Chocolate-Dipped Ginger Shortbread Cookies

The combination of spicy-sweet candied ginger and deep, dark chocolate will truly make your friends squeal with delight. The chocolate-dipping step is a whole lot easier than you'd ever imagine, but if you're really too lazy or you just don't feel like spending the extra time, the cookies are perfectly delicious without the chocolate coating.

1 cup (2 sticks) unsalted butter, softened
1 cup powdered sugar
2 cups all-purpose flour
1 teaspoon vanilla extract
pinch of table salt
¾ cup crystallized ginger, cut into ⅛-inch to ¼-inch dice
8 ounces semisweet or bittersweet baking chocolate, chopped

In a food processor or with an electric mixer, cream butter. Add sugar and continue mixing until combined. Add flour, vanilla, salt, and ginger and mix until dough comes together in a smooth ball. Wrap dough in plastic wrap, forming it into a log about 2 inches in diameter. Refrigerate at least 1 hour and up to three days.

Preheat oven to 300°F.

Remove dough from refrigerator and slice into thin rounds using a very sharp or serrated knife. (Alternatively, dough can be rolled out on a lightly floured board and cut with cookie cutters.) Place cookies ½ inch apart on an ungreased baking sheet. (You may need to bake in batches.) Bake in preheated oven 20 to 30 minutes, until cookies are a very pale golden color. Remove from oven and allow to cool on baking sheet.

Line a baking sheet with parchment paper. Place chopped chocolate in a bowl and microwave on 50 percent power about 2 minutes. Stir with a fork until completely melted. (You may need to microwave it for another 30 to 60 seconds.) Dip cookies in melted chocolate, coating half of each; let the excess drip into the bowl. Place dipped cookies on prepared baking sheet and chill in the fridge until chocolate hardens, about 30 minutes. Store dipped cookies in an airtight container on the countertop.

Makes about 40 cookies.

Make it ahead

Uncooked dough can be stored, tightly wrapped, in the fridge for several days, or in the freezer for up to a month. To freeze, wrap each log tightly in plastic wrap and store in a heavy-duty freezer storage bag. When ready to bake cookies, use a very sharp knife to slice frozen dough into thin rounds and bake as directed above. Baked cookies will keep, stored at room temperature in an airtight container, for several days.

Serve it with

✦ Pink Peppercorn Ice Cream (page 173) or plain chocolate or vanilla ice cream

Change it up

Instead of the candied ginger, mix in:

✦ 1 tablespoon lemon or orange zest
✦ 2 teaspoons ground ginger
✦ ½ cup finely ground pecans
✦ 1 tablespoon instant espresso powder
✦ 2 teaspoons ground cinnamon

HOMEMADE ICE CREAM (NO MACHINE REQUIRED!)

Even if you don't have an ice cream maker, you can still amaze your friends by making your own ice creams and sorbets from scratch. Machines do yield a smooth, creamy result, but you can replicate this effect by hand with a minimal amount of elbow grease. (If you do have an ice cream maker, just mix the ingredients, pour them into the machine, and process according the manufacturer's instructions.)

Lime Dream Ice Cream

Serve this refreshing frozen treat with plain sugar cookies, wafers, or shortbread to temper and complement the tartness of the lime.

> ¾ cup fresh lime juice (from 7 to 9 limes)
> ¾ cup sugar
> grated zest of one lime
> 1½ cups heavy cream

In a small saucepan over medium-low heat, bring the lime juice and sugar to a simmer and cook, stirring, just until sugar dissolves, 1 to 2 minutes. Remove from heat and set aside or place in the refrigerator to cool. Stir in the zest and cream, mix well, pour into a baking dish or shallow bowl, and place in the freezer. After 45 minutes, remove the dish from the freezer and stir the contents vigorously, breaking up any frozen bits. Repeat this process every 30 minutes or so, until ice cream is well frozen, about 4 hours.

Serves 4.

Make it ahead

The ice cream can be kept in the freezer for a few weeks.

Change it up

✦ Substitute lemon or orange juice and zest for the lime, adjusting the sugar as needed to account for the sweeter fruit.

Pink Peppercorn Ice Cream

Pink peppercorns are not actually peppercorns, but the dried berries of an exotic South American rose plant. With an alluring flavor that is pungent, flowery, and slightly sweet, they turn simple ice cream into a mysteriously addictive conversation piece.

2 cups half-and-half
½ cup sugar
2 teaspoons pink peppercorns, crushed

Combine half-and-half, sugar, and crushed peppercorns in a saucepan and bring to a gentle simmer over medium heat. Reduce heat to low and simmer, stirring occasionally, about 5 minutes. Strain through a fine mesh sieve or strainer into a wide, shallow bowl or baking dish and refrigerate several hours or overnight.

Place half-and-half mixture in the freezer. After 45 minutes, remove the dish from the freezer and stir the contents vigorously, breaking up any frozen bits around the edge. Repeat this process every 30 minutes or so, until ice cream is well frozen, about 3 hours.

Serves 4.

Make it ahead

The ice cream can be kept in the freezer for a few weeks.

Serve it with

✦ Miniature Flourless Chocolate Cakes (page 183)
✦ Bittersweet Chocolate Drizzle (page 165)
✦ Chocolate-Dipped Ginger Shortbread Cookies (page 170) or any crunchy cookie

Crème Fraîche and Buttermilk Ice Cream

The creamy, slightly tart flavor of this ice cream is perfect with fruity or chocolate desserts.

1 cup (about 8 ounces) crème fraîche
1 cup buttermilk
½ cup sugar

Mix crème fraîche, buttermilk, and sugar thoroughly in a wide, durable bowl or baking dish and place in the freezer. After 45 minutes, remove the dish from the freezer. At this point the edges should be starting to freeze and the middle should still be slushy. Using a fork or stiff whisk, scrape down the sides of the bowl and stir the contents vigorously, completely breaking up any frozen bits. When mixture is perfectly smooth, return it to the freezer. Repeat this process every 30 minutes or so until the ice cream is well frozen, with a soft, thick texture—about 3 hours.

Serves 4.

Make it ahead

The ice cream can be kept in the freezer for a few weeks.

Serve it with
+ Cherry Clafoutis (page 178)
+ Miniature Flourless Chocolate Cakes (page 183)
+ Fruit tarts
+ Bittersweet Chocolate Drizzle (page 165)
+ Fresh fruit

Pignoli Amaretti

You'll pay a pretty *centesimo* for these nutty little cookies at an Italian bakery. Turns out they're pretty easy to make! Traditional recipes use store-bought almond paste, but we like this version that uses blanched almonds.

    2⅔ cups blanched almonds
    1 cup sugar
    2 tablespoons olive oil
    2 large egg whites
    1⅓ cups pine nuts

Preheat oven to 350°F. Lightly oil a baking sheet.

In a food processor, grind almonds and sugar to a fine powder. Add oil and egg whites and process until batter is well combined.

Form batter into 1-inch balls and roll in pine nuts, pressing the nuts onto the balls. Place balls about 2 inches apart on prepared baking sheet. Bake in preheated oven until lightly browned, 20 to 25 minutes.

Makes 35 to 40 cookies.

Make it ahead

The cookies will keep, stored on the countertop in an airtight container, for up to a week. They'll last even longer in the fridge.

Serve it with

✦ Chocolate gelato and coffee or tea

Pistachio Ice Cream with Strawberries and Balsamic Syrup

If you think strawberries and vinegar sounds like a strange combination, you'll just have to trust us and try this dessert. Highlight the stunning colors by serving this dish in clear glass bowls, or even martini glasses.

¾ pound strawberries, hulled and sliced (about 2 cups)
2 tablespoons sugar
1 pint pistachio ice cream
¼ cup Balsamic Syrup (page 147)

In a medium bowl, mix the strawberries and sugar. Let stand at room temperature, stirring occasionally, until strawberries have softened and become juicy, at least 1 hour and up to 3 hours.

Scoop ice cream into 4 serving bowls or glasses, dividing evenly, and top with the strawberries. Drizzle balsamic syrup over each serving.

Serves 4.

Serve it with
✦ Chocolate-Dipped Ginger Shortbread Cookies (page 170)

Poached Pears with Bittersweet Chocolate Drizzle

Poached pears are a luscious yet simple dessert. They'll satisfy your sweet tooth but won't make you feel overly stuffed after a rich, filling meal. Be sure to use a firm variety of pear, like Bosc or Anjou. If you choose to serve your pears with an optional scoop of ice cream, try pistachio, almond, coconut, or our Crème Fraîche and Buttermilk (page 174) or Pink Peppercorn (page 173).

    6 cups water
    1½ cups sugar
    4 ripe firm pears peeled, halved, and cored
    ice cream for serving (optional)
    Bittersweet Chocolate Drizzle (page 165)

Bring water and sugar to a boil in a stockpot or large saucepan. Place pear halves in water and reduce heat to low. To prevent the pears from bobbing out of the water and cooking unevenly, place a pie tin or a small pot lid in the pot to keep the pears submerged. Depending on the size of your pears, poaching time will vary from about 15 to 30 minutes, so after 15 minutes of simmering check regularly for doneness by discreetly poking a fork into the cut side of one of the pears. Pears are done when they're tender but not mushy. Remove pears from the liquid and let them cool for 5 to 10 minutes.

Pour most of the chocolate drizzle on four serving plates, dividing evenly, reserving a little bit for a final drizzling. Place two pear halves on each plate, cut side down, with one half leaned up against the other in a decorative fashion. Add a scoop of ice cream to each plate, if desired, and drizzle with the remaining chocolate sauce.

Serves 4.

Make it ahead

The pears can be poached a few days ahead and stored in the fridge in an airtight container. Bring to room temperature or pop in the microwave for 1 to 2 minutes before serving.

Cherry Clafoutis

The French name on its own is practically enough to make this dish a winner. *Clafoutis* (claw-foo-tee) is a traditional French dessert that resembles a baked custard, with a moist, dense consistency. Purists insist on leaving the pits in the cherries, because they impart a special flavor as they cook, but there's no shame in not wanting to break a tooth. Go ahead and really flout tradition by substituting any soft fruit you like in place of the cherries, for example, berries, apricots, or plums.

¼ cup (½ stick) unsalted butter, melted
¾ cup sugar
1½ cups whole or low-fat milk
1 cups all-purpose flour
3 large eggs
¼ teaspoon table salt
1 pound (about 3 cups) fresh or frozen cherries, pitted or unpitted
powdered sugar (optional)

Preheat oven to 350°F. Oil an 11 x 7-inch baking dish.

By hand or with a blender, food processor, electric stand mixer, or hand-held mixer, blend butter, sugar, milk, flour, eggs, and salt until batter is smooth and no lumps remain. Place cherries in an even layer in the bottom of the baking dish and pour batter over them. Bake 50 to 60 minutes, until clafoutis is set all the way through and lightly browned on top.

Let cool a few minutes, sprinkle with powdered sugar (if using), and serve warm or at room temperature.

Serves 8 to 12.

Make it ahead

The batter can be made up to a couple of days ahead and stored, covered, in the fridge. Stir well before pouring into the baking dish. Clafoutis is just as good at room temperature a few hours after baking as it is fresh out of the oven. It's even delicious served cold the next day.

Serve it with

✦ Whipped cream, yogurt, or crème fraîche
✦ Crème Fraîche and Buttermilk Ice Cream (page 174)

Change it up

✦ Substitute any soft fruit you like in place of the cherries. Try blueberries, strawberries, apricots, peaches, or plums.

Ricotta with Figs, Almonds, and Honey

This Mediterranean dessert is so jam-packed with healthy ingredients that you'll be surprised by how rich, creamy, and satisfying it is. It's a perfect end to a light summer meal, or even a sweet way to start your day.

2 cups whole-milk ricotta cheese
8–10 medium fresh figs, quartered
⅓ cup toasted unsalted almonds
¼ cup honey

Divide ricotta evenly among 4 dessert plates, followed by the figs and almonds. Drizzle honey on top.

Serves 4.

Change it up

✦ Try this dish with strawberries, blueberries, peaches, pears, or other fruit.
✦ Garnish each serving with a couple of fresh mint leaves.

Lazy Chocolate "Mousse"

We think this divine concoction will throw you for a loop—its smooth, mousse-like consistency is achieved with no egg, no heat, and precious little work. If you're really too lazy to bust out the food processor (or don't have one), you could make this using an electric mixer or even stirring by hand, but you won't get the silky texture that we think is what makes this dessert so dreamy.

2 pounds (about 3½ cups) whole-milk ricotta cheese
1 cup powdered sugar
1 cup heavy cream
½ cup unsweetened cocoa powder
1 teaspoon vanilla extract
sweetened, flaked coconut, for garnish (optional)

Blend ricotta, sugar, cream, cocoa powder, and vanilla in a food processor until smooth. Spoon into eight 4-ounce (½-cup) ramekins, custard cups, Asian-style tea cups, or martini glasses. Cover with plastic wrap and refrigerate until well chilled. Sprinkle with flaked coconut, if using, and serve.

Serves 8.

Make it ahead
The mousse can be kept, covered, in the fridge for a few days.

Serve it with
✦ Crisp sugar cookies or biscotti

Change it up
Replace cocoa powder with:
✦ 2 cups fresh or frozen berries
✦ 2 cups peeled and cubed soft fruit (such as peach or mango)
✦ 2 teaspoons cinnamon

Chocolate Indulgence with Raspberry Coulis

This dense chocolate dessert is extremely rich, so small servings are essential—try serving it in espresso cups, Asian tea cups, shot glasses, or other small dishes. For maximum humor effect, make sure your guest list includes all of your largest, tallest friends.

1 cup heavy cream
8 ounces semisweet chocolate
2 large egg yolks
1 teaspoon vanilla extract
3 tablespoons Raspberry Coulis (page 164), plus more for garnish
1½ tablespoons unsalted butter

In a medium saucepan, heat cream until almost boiling. Remove from heat and stir in chocolate until melted. Add egg yolks, vanilla, and raspberry coulis and stir until smooth. Stir in butter until melted and well combined. Pour into six small (2-ounce) bowls, espresso cups, Asian tea cups, or other small dishes. Chill until firm, at least 2 hours. To serve, drizzle a bit of the raspberry coulis over each dish.

Serves 6.

Make it ahead

The dessert can be stored, covered, in the fridge for a couple of days.

Serve it with

✦ Crunchy sugar cookies, biscotti, or other cookies

Change it up

✦ Replace the raspberry coulis with 3 tablespoons of strong brewed coffee, and serve with a dollop of whipped cream flavored with more coffee.

Chocolate Ricotta Turnovers

These flaky, buttery bundles of melted chocolate, creamy ricotta cheese, and rich pecans are a decadent delight—and they won't take you more than a few minutes to prepare. Be sure to read the section on working with frozen puff pastry (page 14).

⅓ cup ricotta cheese
⅓ cup milk chocolate morsels
⅓ cup chopped toasted pecans
1 tablespoon (packed) brown sugar
1 sheet frozen puff pastry, defrosted
1 large egg, lightly beaten (optional)

Preheat oven to 400°F. Lightly oil a baking sheet.

In a small bowl mix together ricotta, chocolate morsels, pecans, and brown sugar.

Unfold the pastry sheet on a lightly floured surface. Roll the sheet into a 12-inch square using a lightly floured rolling pin. Trim uneven edges, cut sheet into 4 equal squares, and place squares on prepared baking sheet. Place ricotta mixture in the center of each pastry square, dividing evenly.

Brush a little water around the edges of each pastry square to make them sticky. Fold each square into a triangle, sealing the damp edges together by pressing firmly. For a shiny glaze, if desired, brush egg lightly over the tops.

Bake 15 to 20 minutes, until pastry is golden brown and nicely puffed up. Serve warm.

Makes 4 turnovers.

Make it ahead

Turnovers are best served right out of the oven, but if you want to enjoy them as leftovers you can store them in the fridge, covered, for a couple of days. Reheat at 400°F until heated through (about 5 minutes).

Serve it with

✦ A dollop of whipped cream or a drizzle of Raspberry Coulis (page 164)

Change it up

✦ Add 2 tablespoons chopped candied orange rind to the ricotta mixture.

Miniature Flourless Chocolate Cakes

Our time-tested credo "Just put it in a ramekin" proves itself once again with this rich, decadent, thoroughly delicious dessert. You can easily convince your guests that you spent all day in the kitchen making them (as long as you don't slip up and start talking about the fascinating paternity tests you saw on the all-day *Maury Povich Show* marathon).

    4 ounces bittersweet or semisweet baking chocolate, chopped
    ½ cup (1 stick) unsalted butter
    ¾ cup sugar
    ½ cup unsweetened cocoa powder
    pinch of table salt
    3 large eggs
    1 teaspoon vanilla extract
    ice cream or whipped cream for serving (optional)

Preheat oven to 375°F. Grease six 4-ounce (½-cup) ramekins with spray oil, vegetable oil, or butter.

In a microwave-safe bowl large enough to hold all the ingredients, microwave the butter and chocolate 30 seconds. Stir well and microwave another 30 seconds. Continue stirring and microwaving until butter and chocolate are completely melted and thoroughly combined. Stir in sugar, cocoa powder, salt, eggs, and vanilla and mix thoroughly.

Place ramekins on a baking sheet to allow for easier transfer in and out of the oven, and divide batter evenly among them. Bake in preheated oven for 25 to 30 minutes, until the cakes look tall and puffy and a toothpick inserted into the center comes out almost clean. (If you prefer drier cakes, you can leave them in the oven a few minutes longer, until a toothpick inserted into the center comes out completely clean and dry.)

Serve warm (after allowing to cool a little bit), right in the ramekins or unmolded onto small plates, with a scoop of ice cream or a dollop of whipped cream.

Serves 6.

Serve it with
   + Crème Fraîche and Buttermilk Ice Cream (page 174) or Pink Peppercorn Ice Cream (page 173)
   + Store-bought ice cream, any flavor
   + A dollop of whipped cream or crème fraîche
   + A drizzle of Raspberry Coulis (page 164)
   + A sprig of mint

Orange Crème Fraîche Cake with Bittersweet Chocolate Drizzle

We always wanted to be the type of people who could whip up a scrumptious cake on a moment's notice. That's why we developed this recipe for a cake that can be stirred together in one bowl and tossed into the oven. Rich, creamy crème fraîche makes it incredibly moist, and lots of orange zest and orange juice give it intense orange flavor. A quick bittersweet chocolate glaze is the final touch that made us realize that this cake was The One (and yes, we would marry it if we could). We recommend a Bundt pan for maximum visual appeal, but a springform pan or a simple round cake pan will do as well.

1 cup crème fraîche
⅔ cup vegetable oil
1 cup sugar
grated zest of 2 large oranges
¼ cup fresh squeezed orange juice (from about 1 orange)
2 tablespoons lemon juice (from about ½ lemon)
1½ teaspoons vanilla extract
3 large eggs
1½ cups all-purpose flour
1½ teaspoons baking powder
½ teaspoon baking soda
½ teaspoon table salt
Bittersweet Chocolate Drizzle (page 165)

Preheat oven to 350°F. Oil or butter a 10-inch Bundt pan or 9-inch round cake or springform pan.

In a large mixing bowl, whisk together crème fraîche, oil, sugar, orange zest, orange juice, lemon juice, and vanilla. Add eggs and whisk until incorporated. Add flour, baking powder, baking soda, and salt and whisk until just combined. (Don't worry if there are small lumps; you don't want to overmix this cake or it will become dry.)

Pour batter into prepared pan and bake in preheated oven for 30 to 40 minutes, until the top is golden brown and a toothpick inserted into the center comes out clean. Remove cake from oven, place the pan on a wire rack, and let cool for 15 minutes.

Remove the cake from the pan by running a knife around the side of the pan and inverting it directly onto the wire rack. (If you've baked the cake in a flat-bottomed round cake pan rather than a Bundt pan, invert the cake onto the rack and flip it over so that the bottom of the cake, not the top, is resting on the wire rack—otherwise you'll end up with unattractive indentations from the cooling rack on the top.) Let cool completely. Transfer to a large plate or cake platter before glazing.

When cake is completely cooled, drizzle the chocolate glaze over it until covered to your liking (you may have extra glaze left over) and let sit at room temperature at least 1 hour before serving. Serve at room temperature.

Serves 12.

Make it ahead

The cake can be made and glazed 24 hours ahead and kept, uncovered, on the countertop. When the cake has been cut, cover with foil or plastic wrap and keep on the countertop for a couple of days.

Change it up

✦ Instead of one large cake, make cupcakes using a cupcake or muffin tin. Reduce cooking time to about 25 minutes (or until a toothpick inserted into the center comes out clean).

✦ Instead of chocolate glaze, make an orange glaze by stirring together 1 cup powdered sugar and about 3 tablespoons (more if needed to make a smooth glaze) fresh-squeezed orange juice (from about ½ large orange).

✦ Replace the orange zest and juice with the zest and juice of 1 large lemon or 2 small limes (leaving out the additional tablespoon of lemon juice) and glaze with a mixture of 1 cup powdered sugar and about 3 tablespoons (more if needed to make a smooth glaze) lemon or lime juice.

✦ Make a rich chocolate version of the cake by leaving out the lemon juice (the orange zest and juice can be left in for a chocolate-orange version or left out for a straight chocolate version) and adding ⅔ cup unsweetened cocoa powder with the other dry ingredients. Glaze with the orange glaze above or the bittersweet chocolate glaze.

Bananas Bread Pudding Foster

Heavenly, rich, indescribably decadent—Bananas Bread Pudding Foster is not for the faint of heart. Consult your doctor, confess your sins, and go for it. (And don't forget to invite us. We *really* like this dessert.)

¼ cup (½ stick) unsalted butter, softened
¾ cup (packed) brown sugar
2 large eggs
1¼ cups whole milk
½ cup half-and-half
½ cup bourbon or other whiskey
1 teaspoon vanilla extract
½ loaf (about 8 ounces) dense, mildly flavored white bread (with crust left on),
    such as Italian, French, brioche, or Pullman loaf (not sourdough), cubed
3 bananas, sliced

In a large bowl, cream together butter and sugar with an electric mixer. Beat in eggs, milk, half-and-half, bourbon, and vanilla. (Batter may be somewhat lumpy, which is okay.) Stir in bread and bananas.

Preheat oven to 350°F.

Pour batter into a 9 x 9-inch baking dish. Cover and refrigerate 2 to 8 hours to allow the bread to soak up the liquid. Bake in preheated oven, uncovered, 75 to 90 minutes, until top is golden brown. Let sit at least 5 minutes before serving.

Serves 6 to 8.

Change it up
+ Add ½ cup raisins with the bananas and bread.
+ Substitute cinnamon-raisin bread or challah for the white bread.
+ For added crunch, after the pudding has been in the oven about 70 minutes, sprinkle with ½ cup chopped pecans and continue baking another 20 minutes.
+ Instead of making one large bread pudding, bake in 8 individual 4-ounce (½-cup) ramekins or custard cups for 60 to 75 minutes, or until tops are golden brown.

ACKNOWLEDGMENTS

We'd like to thank our families—especially Doug and Cashel Reil; Tom and Shirley Donovan; Dahlia, Andres, and Sissel Ramirez; and Janet Gallin and Ted Kelter—for being stalwart tasters of our Lazy Gourmet experiments, both delicious and not so, and for supporting us in countless other ways.

We are deeply grateful for the unflagging enthusiasm, diligence, and hard work of Brenda Knight, Frédérique Delacoste, Felice Newman, Mark Rhynsburger, Scott Idleman, Kara Wuest, Bridget Kinsella, Kat Sanborn, and the whole Viva Editions team. We also wish to thank Jeevan Sivasubramanian and Anthony Tassinello for their sage wisdom and advice; Joanne Weir for her kind words and support; and Sarah Rosenberg, Kim Wylie, Elise Cannon, Dave Dahl, and the entire Publishers Group West crew for their invaluable expertise.

Finally, we give the hugest possible thank-you to our army of volunteer recipe testers—the regular home cooks who helped ensure that every single recipe we developed for this book passed our strict tests of easiness, deliciousness, and impressiveness. We could not have done this without their constant encouragement and, most important, rigorous feedback.

So, special thanks to:

Edith Allgood
Kendra Armer
Eli Ateljevich
Nancy Botkin
Aneela Brister
Linda Carson
Linda Chu
Michelle Contey
Betsy Cordes
Frank D'Amico
Jason Dewees
Shirley Donovan
Colin Duwe
Tresa Eyres

Janet Gallin
Laura Lee Gillespie
Bethany Gladhill
Sarah Kate Heilbrun
Shelley Kazliner
Toni Lambert
Laurie Lanquist
Carrie Laurent
Tiffany Lee
Diane Leon
Shana Lindsay
Rosanne Lurie
Jean Ann Luther
Julie Malork

Robin Marks
Kim McCauley
Sue McIntire
Jennifer McKee
Carolyn Meyer
Bonnie Monte
Lynn Tabb Noyce
Pamela Nudel
Andres Ramirez
Dahlia Gallin Ramirez
Lucia Bustamante Reavely
Greg Robb
Sara Robb
Carol Rooney

David Rosenthal
Paul Schreiber
Colin Sjostedt
Mike Smith
Valerie Sobel
Kappy Sugawara
Mark Sweeney
Linda Vegher
Anthony Vento
Richard Wagner
Laura Wasserman
Cheryl Wilson
Makiko Wisner

ACKNOWLEDGMENTS ABOUT THE AUTHORS

ABOUT THE AUTHORS

Juliana Gallin and Robin Donovan
Andres Ramirez, aprphotography.com

ROBIN DONOVAN is the author of *Campfire Cuisine: Gourmet Recipes for the Great Outdoors* and coauthor of the *New York Times* bestseller *Dr. Gott's No Flour, No Sugar Diet.* Her food writing has appeared in *Cooking Light, Fitness, San Jose Mercury News, Seattle Post-Intelligencer,* www.Sallys-Place.com, *San Francisco Chronicle*, and other publications.

Robin knows her way around a kitchen—and has even been known to devote hours to creating exceedingly elaborate dishes—but with a busy writing schedule and an even busier kid, she has to rely on quick, simple recipes if she wants keep up appearances with her foodie friends.

JULIANA GALLIN is the poster girl for Lazy Gourmets. She loves to delight friends and family with magnificent meals, but always aims to avoid complicated, time-consuming, dish-dirtying culinary labors. Her bottom line is that she values flavor, surprise, and sophistication in her cooking, but not if it means having to miss *Hoarders.*

When she's not cooking effortless gourmet feasts, or writing books about how to cook effortless gourmet feasts, Juliana works as a graphic designer and produces several popular speakers' series in San Francisco, including Ask a Scientist, How-To Night, and Comedy Talks.

Robin and Juliana met as college housemates in Santa Cruz, California. An early, ill-fated culinary collaboration—a terribly misguided sauté of *nopales* (a Mexican cactus)—failed to discourage their friendship or their teamwork in the kitchen. More than 20 years later, both living in the San Francisco Bay Area, they continue to cook and eat together regularly, sharing recipes, ideas, successes, and still the occasional culinary disaster. Read their food blog at www.twolazygourmets.com.

MEASUREMENT CONVERSION CHARTS

DRY VOLUME MEASUREMENTS

MEASURE	EQUIVALENT
$^1/_{16}$ teaspoon	dash
$^1/_8$ teaspoon	a pinch
3 teaspoons	1 tablespoon
$^1/_8$ cup	2 tablespoons (= 1 standard coffee scoop)
$^1/_4$ cup	4 tablespoons
$^1/_3$ cup	5 tablespoons plus 1 teaspoon
$^1/_2$ cup	8 tablespoons
$^3/_4$ cup	12 tablespoons
1 cup	16 tablespoons
1 pound	16 ounces

LIQUID VOLUME MEASUREMENTS

8 fluid ounces	1 cup
1 pint	2 cups (= 16 fluid ounces)
1 quart	2 pints (= 4 cups)
1 gallon	4 quarts (= 16 cups)

U.S. TO METRIC CONVERSIONS

$^1/_5$ teaspoon	1 ml (milliliter)
1 teaspoon	5 ml
1 tablespoon	15 ml
1 fluid ounce	30 ml
$^1/_5$ cup	50 ml
1 cup	240 ml
2 cups (1 pint)	470 ml
4 cups (1 quart)	.95 liter
4 quarts (1 gallon)	3.8 liters
1 ounce	28 grams
1 pound	454 grams

METRIC TO U.S. CONVERSIONS

1 ml (milliliter)	⅕ teaspoon
5 ml	1 teaspoon
15 ml	1 tablespoon
30 ml	1 fluid ounce
100 ml	3.4 fluid ounces
240 ml	1 cup
1 liter	34 fluid ounces
1 liter	4.2 cups
1 liter	2.1 pints
1 liter	1.06 quarts
1 liter	.26 gallon
1 gram	.035 ounce
100 grams	3.5 ounces
500 grams	1.10 pounds
1 kilogram	2.205 pounds
1 kilogram	35 ounces

PAN SIZE EQUIVALENTS

9 x 13-inch baking dish	22 x 33 cm (centimeter)
8 x 8-inch baking dish	20 x 20 cm
9 x 5-inch loaf pan	23 x 12 cm loaf tin
10-inch tart or cake pan	25 cm
9-inch cake pan	22 cm

FARENHEIT	CELSIUS	GAS MARK
275°F	140°C	gas mark 1–cool
300°F	150°C	gas mark 2
325°F	165°C	gas mark 3–very moderate
350°F	180°C	gas mark 4–moderate
375°F	190°C	gas mark 5
400°F	200°C	gas mark 6–moderately hot
425°F	220°C	gas mark 7–hot
450°F	230°C	gas mark 9
475°F	240°C	gas mark 10–very hot

INDEX

TO OUR READERS

Viva Editions publishes books that inform, enlighten, and entertain. We do our best to bring you, the reader, quality books that celebrate life, inspire the mind, revive the spirit, and enhance lives all around. Our authors are practical visionaries: people who offer deep wisdom in a hopeful and helpful manner. Viva was launched with an attitude of growth and we want to spread our joy and offer our support and advice where we can to help you live the Viva way: vivaciously!

We're grateful for all our readers and want to keep bringing you books for inspired living. We invite you to write to us with your comments and suggestions, and what you'd like to see more of. You can also sign up for our online newsletter to learn about new titles, author events, and special offers.

Viva Editions
2246 Sixth St.
Berkeley, CA 94710
www.vivaeditions.com
(800) 780-2279
Follow us on Twitter @vivaeditions
Friend/fan us on Facebook